Over the course of the year various jobs must be done in the garden. Some are tied to the season, but many continue throughout the entire growing season.

SPRING

SUMMER

WOLFGANG HENSEL

GARDENING
for Beginners

**Successful Gardening—
How to Do It
Important Chores
Step by Step**

**More than 350 color photographs
by Ursel Borstell, Wolfgang Redeleit,
Jürgen Becker, Marion Nickig, and
other garden photographers**

**Illustrations by
Renate Holzner**

Contents

Designing Gardens

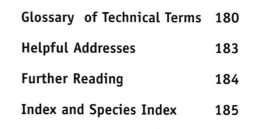

Garden Care

The Prerequisites

Designing and caring for a garden as a personal living space is one of the most beautiful and satisfying leisure time activities.

With some basic knowledge, much enthusiasm, and commitment, any plot of land can be turned into an appealing, very personal garden.

Constructing a Garden

Constructing a garden demands a certain expenditure of planning and practical work. The more precise you can be about your wants and the options you have before you start, the more likely the result will match your expectations.

Creating a garden can be roughly broken down into four steps:
1. What type of garden do you want? Are you prepared to do regular maintenance chores, or do you want a lower-maintenance garden?
2. What possibilities does your plot offer? On a flat surface, the size of the garden alone governs the design options. But if the surface is sloping or very shady, you must also take these features into consideration.
3. How should the garden be designed? You should divide the available surface area artfully and let choice of color and form bring the various parts of the garden to optimal effect.
4. What jobs are required? This has to do with the plants and the regular care of the garden.

Try to see if you can follow these steps.

The Procedure

An empty plot of ground can be turned into the garden of your dreams step by step—beginning with planning. On the other hand, old gardens contain structures already grown, which lend the area a certain maturity from the start. Here it becomes a matter of integrating the elements already present into your own concept, or removing undesired walls, paths, trees, and shrubs. Before you pick up a spade, or select plants for your garden, read through the following pages.

A garden with a pond and borders requires relatively more care—it is also particularly beautiful.

What Do I Want?

In advance of any planning, every "green" garden owner should be clear about what kind of garden he or she wants. This determines the design as well as the choice of plants and, above all, the amount of care that will be required to maintain it. An intensively used yard with a place for barbecuing and play equipment for the children will look entirely different than a yard that is dominated by flowering perennials.

Anyone who enjoys keeping busy and doing physical labor in the garden—perhaps even growing some edible plants for the table—will certainly have a different kind of garden than a garden owner who prefers to let his thoughts wander in a comfortable armchair or chaise lounge.

The Lawn-Accented Garden
A garden with a more or less large lawn area demands the least attention. Once the lawn has been established, the need for care stays within reasonable limits—leaving much time for "lazing." By using lawn in combination with borders, you achieve maximum gardening pleasure with minimum expenditure of effort. However, since a homogeneous green lawn surface can quickly become boring, you should "play" with the shape of the lawn. Slanting or curving edges are more interesting than straight edges. A tree or large shrub,

an arbor or pergola, or sculpture provide interesting focal points.

The Shrub-Accented Garden
The idea of a shrub hedge is already found in the origins of the word *garden,* which goes back to the Indogermanic *ghorto* or *ghordo,* not referring to the surface but to the boundaries of the garden. Almost every gardener has felt the irresistable urge to enclose his or her domain with a fence or a screening or privacy hedge. If the hedge consists of various kinds of staggered tall shrubs, a shrub-accented garden results. As with grass, the amount of effort required is small. If you choose shrubs that bloom at different times, develop colorful fruits, and/or develop good fall color, a shrubbery border is an adequate substitute for a perennial border.

Livening up with Tub Plants
Container plantings can provide extra flower and green foliage color throughout the garden.

If the garden is large enough, shrubs can be planted in islands with beautiful flowers that draw the eye to them. At the same time, hidden spaces develop behind them, contributing to the structuring of the garden.

Cottage Gardens and Kitchen Gardens
Extravagant, lush flower display, together with edible plants and herbs—that's how the cottage garden looks. In the cottage garden there is no space for a lawn—if need be, an arbor at the end of the path invites a pause.

Cottage gardens are, however, very maintenance-intensive. They may only be neglected for a short time before they go wild and look awful: vegetables need to be sown, cared for, and harvested; the perennials must be regularly divided and cut back. Consider that a "real" kitchen garden, with crossing paths and a central bed requires much space (at least 215 ft^2 or 20 m^2). In large properties, set off an appropriate area with a hedge (e.g., of berry bushes) and a vine-clad arch. In smaller yards, a cottage garden bed with flowering perennials represents a good compromise.

The Border-Accented Garden
A splendidly blooming perennial border certainly is one of the most

Perennial beds or flower borders demand the most planning and care.

beautiful visions that a garden can offer. The work required is, however, even greater than that for kitchen and cottage gardens. A border demands targeted planning in the selection of plants. The plants must be chosen according to flower color, blooming season, and growth form to keep the bed looking attractive throughout the entire growing season. First decide on a simple color scheme (tone on tone)—such beds are easier to design than multicolored areas.

While it is acceptable for cottage gardens to look a little "wild"—that's even part of their charm—the plants in a border should be in optimal condition.

Therefore, of all the garden types, a garden with flower borders needs the most planning, the greatest expenditure of effort, and consistent maintenance.

Before you get into the details of planning, decide which criteria are most important to you. You can adopt a particular garden type entirely or only make use of certain elements of it. Gardens that use various styles can be very interesting.

EXPERT TIP
The more lavish the garden, the more work it takes.

CROSS-REFERENCES
Seeding lawns pages 38–41
Planting shrubs pages 46–47

What Do I Have?

Whichever type of garden you want to create, it is dependent on the features of your property as well as those of your adjacent neighbors' property. Thus, something like a beautiful tree in your neighbor's yard becomes a visual element of your own garden when you blur the boundary with a shrubbery border.

The City Garden

Small back courts, interior courtyards, or narrow strips along the building are suitable for a garden. The obvious disadvantages—small areas, shadowy areas, limiting walls—can be turned into something positive. Treat the garden area as a kind of "outdoor living room." Create a place to sit with natural stones, flags, gravel, or a wooden deck. Cloak the bordering walls with green and choose small, robust shrubs or hardy perennials. Structure the surface with raised beds of differing heights, and also use areas above ground level.

The Detached or Row House Garden

The areas available for a detached or row house garden are usually limited. Therefore, before you

separate yourself from your neighbor by a dense hedge of evergreens, you should definitely consider other possibilities, such as:
▶ A staggered shrub border or skillfully placed, wide-spreading shrubs have a much more interesting effect than the uniform green of conifers.
▶ Trellises, green-clad pergolas, or tall growing shrubs placed directly in

Privet hedges can be kept relatively narrow and offer good privacy.

front of the terrace protect the sitting area from passersby.
▶ In small gardens install contouring dividers and focal points (rose arbors, vine-covered rail gates, groups of shrubs) to create interest and a feeling of spaciousness.
▶ Put in curving and scalloped lawn areas.

The Large Garden

In rural and outer suburban areas, you can still find relatively affordable, larger properties.
▶ In gardens of this sort, take the landscape into consideration: Direct the eye with trees, shrubs, or overgrown arches and gates, avenue-like, to a beautiful group of trees or garden ornamentation.

Thus the garden will look spacious and wider.
▶ It should be impossible to see the whole of a large garden from one spot. Therefore, create rooms with green "walls"—hedges, shrub borders, groups of bushes—or with structures like arches, pergolas, covered passages, and trellises.
▶ Plan an additional sitting area.

Even the smallest and shadiest inner courtyard can become a green oasis with artful plant choice and pots and tubs of plants.

The Sloping Garden

A sloping or hilly lot need not be a disadvantage. If the land slopes toward the house, you can cut it back in terraces (brick or natural stone walls, wooden palisades) or, insofar as the land permits, leave it in its natural slope.

▶ If the angle of decline is steeper than 7%, you must install stairs or steps in a sloping garden.

▶ Don't try to hide the slope, rather, use it as a design element with steps, stairs, and landings.

▶ Select plants that flow down the slope and supporting walls in cascades, and choose shrubs with spreading growth forms.

▶ If the slope falls away from the house, achieve the same effect with a place for sitting at the end of the garden.

▶ Soil often is acidic under conifer hedges, especially if they have been there for years. Plants like azaleas, rhododendrons, or heaths and heathers will grow well here.

▶ Ugly walls can usually be covered with vines—however, you must discuss it with your neighbor first.

Problem Spots

An ever recurring problem with new or renovated gardens is that of the already-existing walls, buildings, or solid fences of the neighbors.

▶ Sun-loving plants will not thrive in the shade of buildings and hedges; here you have to fall back on shade-loving plants.

▶ In the wind shelter of walls or compact hedges, dryness predominates so choose plants that can tolerate it.

Garden Types for Every Location

Garden Type	Location	Design Tips
Lawn garden	Slope	Shrubs and supporting walls as decorative elements
	Detached house	Grass area structured by curving shrub borders
	Row house	Look for interesting lawn shapes
Kitchen garden	Large garden	Separate with hedges and gates
	Detached or row house	Install a cottage garden border
Shrub border	City garden	Tub plants for the open area
	Slope	Be careful to leave open spaces between the shrubs
	Detached or row house	Open hedges of shrubs
Border gardens	City gardens	Shade borders with ferns and wildflowers
	Large gardens	Design borders to be very visible, especially from the sitting area
	Detached or row house	Preferably make one large rather than several small borders

EXPERT TIP
Plan sitting areas on old play surfaces.

CROSS-REFERENCES
Creating rooms pages 158–159
Sitting areas in the garden 178–179

Basic Gardening Equipment

Equipment	You Need	Use and Tips
	**Digging tools** Spade; spading fork; shovel; hoe (for very hard soil).	Spades (with a T-handle or D-handle for easier handling) for turning up soil and cutting edges of beds. Shovel for spreading soil or sand, turning compost. Buy two spading forks if you regularly divide perennials.
	**Tools for working the soil** Hook; rakes; grubber or cultivator.	These implements do heavy work, so make absolutely certain they are of good quality. Hook for loosening soil; rake for smoothing the grass seed; grubber or cultivator for loosening the soil.
	**Tool system** Long handle; in addition, tools for working the soil that can be snapped onto it.	Tool systems offer a great space advantage. With short and long handles (one each), they can be used for everything and replace the corresponding single, fixed tool.
	**Small tools** Trowel; dibble; bulb planter; hand grubber; hand weeder.	Small tools are needed for the kneeling work in the garden or planting bulbs. Make sure that they fit into your hand well. Hand grubbers are ideal for weeding in small areas.

Choose quality products. The extra cost is worth it, for the tools ought to last you many years.

Equipment	You Need	Use and Tips

Pruning tools
Pruning knife (bush hook); hedge cutters (manual or power-operated); clippers with long handles; tree saw; two pairs of pruning shears.

One pair of pruners for small branches, one for perennials. Heavier branches are cut with clippers or the tree saw (smooth the edges of the wound with the bush hook).

Watering equipment
Hose with wall holder or a carrier (also a watering system); sprinkler for the lawn; watering can with fine spray.

Hose carriers are practical, especially in a large garden. With systems an adjustable nozzle and sprinkler wand replace the former.

Lawn care implements
Lawn mower; broom rake; string edger (manual or power); edge cutter (if necessary a spade will do it).

The lawn mower (with grass catcher) should be appropriate for the lawn area. Power mowers are only economical for large areas. Broom rakes or rakes for tidying.

In addition
Gloves; stakes and string; labels; baskets and plastic trash barrels for waste; baling wire; wheelbarrow.

Wear protective gloves for garden work. Keep your implements in a sturdy basket so they all stay together.

Jobs That Have to Be Done

Information in Brief

What Takes How Long?

Watering:
Amount of time depends on the size of the garden

Digging:
About 20 minutes per square yard

Planting perennials:
About 10 minutes per plant

Dividing perennials:
About 10 minutes per plant

Pruning shrubs:
About 30–60 minutes, depending on size

Planting shrubs:
About 30–60 minutes per shrub

When Certain Jobs Have to Be Done

Spring:
Digging, planting perennials and hardy annuals, fertilizing, pruning shrubs, removing spent flowers (deadheading), weeding, mulching

Summer:
Watering, deadheading, fertilizing, planting tender annuals, weeding

Fall:
Planting bulbs, shrubs, and perennials; dividing and cutting back perennials, mulching for winter protection

Digging
Regular digging alters the natural soil structure. Now and then every garden owner must take up the spade if he or she wants to make a new bed and/or add organic matter to improve structure and fertility of an existing bed.

Planting Perennials
How often this job has to be done depends on the gardener's personal preferences. Choose long-lived plants if you dislike this job. However, from time to time, overage perennials should be replaced with new ones or divided. Keen gardeners with an aesthetic bent improve their summer beds with additional annuals anyway. In these situations you must take up the trowel or spade more often.

Some garden chores recur regularly; others recur less often. Familiarize yourself with the most important jobs.

Planting Trees and Shrubs

Most woody plants will survive the garden owner. So it is that much more important to plan this work step precisely, since every tree and bush may remain in the same location for decades. Does the woody plant have enough room to reach its optimum height and breadth? What effect will its increasing shade area have? Mark the position and diameter on a plan. Put a chair in the proposed place. Does the "tree" fit into the garden?

Watering and Fertilizing

No garden owner can avoid doing these jobs, for mineral nutrients and water are the basic necessities for plant growth. When the sun blazes down and the weather report promises no change in sight, you should provide your plants with water in the cool evening hours. Whether you use the watering can, sprinkler, or hose depends on the size of the area. Wet the soil deeply and thoroughly (loosen crusted soil).

As to fertilizers, it is preferable to choose organic products (such as composted manure, humus), since they give up their nutrients slowly and continually, and apply inorganic fertilizers sparingly.

Pruning Plants

Pruning tender and woody plants is a necessary maintenance chore that keeps your garden "in shape." Without pruning, your garden will quickly turn into a wilderness, and fall short from an aesthetic point of view. Besides removing dead or overgrown branches, pruning encourages the shrubs and trees to put out new shoots. Regular removal of spent flowers (deadheading) from perennials and annuals stimulates the plant to produce new flowers.

EXPERT TIP
*Mark the important jobs
on the calendar.*

CROSS-REFERENCES
*Planting plants pages 34–55
Pruning techniques pages 70–75*

Preparing the Soil

The soil is your garden's most important "capital." It must be carefully maintained and improved as necessary.

The various processes of plant growth take place in the soil. It forms the foundation for the roots, which anchor the plant firmly in the ground. Plants also take in water and nutrients through their roots. Therefore, every gardener should have as much precise information about the soil quality of his or her garden as possible.

Soil Quality

The simple crumbling test can determine whether the soil is clayish, loamy, or sandy.

▶ Clay soils retain water and nutrients but they are hard to work.

▶ Sandy soils are easy to work but don't retain water and nutrients.

▶ Normal garden soils are a mixture of clay and sandy elements. Such soils offer the ideal combination: They are relatively easy to work and they store water and nutrients well.

Before you start, you should have a soil analysis performed. Garden centers sell simple testing kits for this purpose. This analysis can be performed by a government cooperative extension agency or private institution that performs soil tests for a fee.

Most garden plants like a soil pH that is slightly acidic (i.e., 6.3–6.8). Regular testing of soil pH every few years is recommended to ensure pH levels are kept in the optimal range. If you need to raise pH, use lime; to lower pH, use sulfur. Refer to your soil test results to determine how much of these materials you may need. Both lime and sulfur are available at most garden centers.

It's a good idea to test the soil a few weeks after applying the materials to see if you've reached your desired pH value.

Soil Maintenance

You achieve good soil fertility when you regularly work in compost. But weeding is also part of good soil care. Weeds take up water and nutrients from the soil that your ornamental plants urgently need. Tall, vigorous weeds also compete with your ornamentals for light.

Soil maintenance does not mean digging. This work is only required with beds that are new or entirely done over. Afterwards, loosening the surface of the soil with a hook or grubber is enough.

To achieve lush flowering and a rich harvest, the soil has to be well maintained.

Fertilizing and Watering

Plants are living things and need nutrients. Unlike animals, however, they are able to use simple inorganic elements to produce organic material on their own, which is why they manage with water and minerals.

Fertilizing, Yes or No?

Why fertilize, since in nature, plants are not fertilized? Gardens are not natural plant communities but "artificial" nature. Biological environments are circulatory systems, in which the plants and animals form the links of an unending chain of recycling. Entirely different conditions prevail in the garden: We want to have lush growth of flowers, shrubs, and trees, possibly even several plant generations in the same location, to harvest fruit and vegetables and mow the lawn—and all this withdraws organic material from circulation. We have to close this "gap" in the circulatory system by fertilizing.

So it is important to supply the soil with a basic provision of organic fertilizer, which adds nutrients slowly. Perennial or vegetable beds that are intensively planted are often given extra fertilizer in the form of inorganic fertilizers. But in moderation! Every plant has only a certain growth potential; thus, overfertilizing might even be injurious and pollute the groundwater supply.

The Basic Table of Nutrients

Among the most important nutrients are nitrogen, phosphorus, potassium, calcium, and magnesium.

▶ Nitrogen (N) is the most important soil nutrient. It is contained in all proteins and is an important element of chlorophyll, which gives leaves their green color. Light-green leaves are a typical sign of nitrogen deficiency. Too much nitrogen, on the other hand, leads to plants becoming too succulent and susceptible to disease.

▶ Phosphorus (P) is also a component of plant protein and plays an important role in energy metabolism. In contrast to nitrogen, phosphorus is not leached away by rain.

▶ Potassium (K) is used by the plants for the development of their cell walls and thus provides for a stable structure.

Water—the Alpha and Omega of Plant Care

Most important, newly planted plants must be well watered.

▶ Calcium or lime (Ca) improves the structure of the soil. It has a neutralizing effect on soil acids and, like potassium, is used in cell walls. Too much calcium in the soil can limit the uptake of trace elements.

▶ Magnesium (Mg) is a component of chlorophyll and thus is important for the plant's energy supply.

Besides these chief nutrients there are also trace elements (e.g., sulfur, iron, copper, zinc), that are only needed in the smallest quantities.

Plants get all other building blocks out of the air. They "breathe in" carbon dioxide (CO_2) and use the sun's energy to build organic molecules from it. This biochemical reaction gives off oxygen (O_2).

Organic and Inorganic Fertilizers

Inorganic (mineral) fertilizers and organic fertilizers contain the same chemical components, but the former work faster and must be manufactured chemically, with consumption of energy.

▶ An inorganic complete fertilizer (chloride-free) contains N, P, and K.

▶ Single fertilizers, on the other hand, consist of only one nutrient and should only be used on the advice of an expert after a soil test.

▶ Animal manures, the best organic fertilizers, are unfortunately not available to everyone (often garden centers offer composted manure).

Rain water is particularly good for watering—it is temperate and lime-free.

▶ Horn, blood, kelp, bone, and cottonseed meal can be applied directly to the bed and then lightly worked into the soil.

▶ Although not fertilizers in the real sense, compost also furnishes the soil with nutrients, and mulch helps improve soil structure.

Watering Correctly

A sufficient supply of water is one of the basic requirements of a plant. When you notice leaves drooping during periods of low rainfall, you must resort to hose or watering can.

▶ Never water in the sun—drops of water on the leaves intensify the effect of sunlight and can burn the leaves—water only in the evening or in the morning.

▶ Try to spray a fine stream of water (adjustable nozzle) directly onto the ground, if possible, until the soil is water-saturated.

▶ Use the watering can to water individual plants.

Expert Tip
Fertilize sparingly, not "the more the better."

Cross-Reference
Composting pages 32–33

Recognizing and Pulling Weeds

Weed Species	Characteristics	Combatting and Tips
	**Goutweed** Perennial; up to 35 in (90 cm) tall and wide; leaves 2–4 in (5–10 cm) long, trifoliate; small, white flowers in an umbrella-like cluster.	Goutweed has a branching, sturdy root system and can't simply be pulled out. Dig out the root with a spading fork and remove new sprouts.
	**Common Quack Grass** Perennial grass; up to 36 in (91 cm) wide and tall; leaves in bunches; brownish green heads in summer to fall.	The rootstock (rhizome) spreads wide and must be completely removed (spading fork). New plants grow from any remaining pieces of root! Mulch heavily.
	Shepherd's Purse Annual; 8–18 in (20–45 cm) tall and wide; gray-green, narrow leaves in a rosette close to the ground; insignificant flowers.	Pull out the young plants by hand (before they bloom, if possible). With older plants, use a hoe to loosen the soil.
	**Bindweed** Perennial; up to 30 in (75 cm) wide, shoots creep or climb; leaves arrow-shaped, 1 in (2.5 cm) long; red-and-white-striped flowers.	Very difficult weed, since the roots are easily torn by pulling. Remove all the pieces of root from the soil, since new plants develop from them.
	**Annual Bluegrass** Annual grass; up to 12 in (30 cm) tall; leaves narrow, bright-green; greenish to brownish yellow flowers in individual panicles.	This little grass keeps sowing itself. Only regular weeding helps with this, since it is hardly possible to remove the grass entirely.

**Not all wild plants are "bad" plants.
Daisies in a field or woodland plants
under shrubs are very attractive.**

Weed Species	Characteristics	Combatting and Tips
	**Creeping Crowfoot or Creeping Buttercup** Perennial; 12 in (30 cm) wide, 20 in (50 cm) tall; three-lobed leaves; bright-yellow flowers.	Crowfoot puts out runners that root quickly and develop new plants. Follow the runners and dig out all roots with a trowel.
	**Sowthistle** Annual; up to 72 in (180 cm) tall, about 8 in (20 cm) wide; small leaves with a lobed or serrated edge; pale-yellow flower heads.	Pull out the young plants as quickly as possible. Luckily it takes a little longer for the plants to bloom and go to seed—so you can maintain good control.
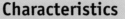	**Chickweed** Annual; creeping to upright, up to 14 in (35 cm) high, 18 in (45 cm) wide; tiny white flowers (all-season).	Simply cut off the chickweed that is climbing on plants and then next day just carefully untangle the wilted weed.
	**Dandelion** Perennial; up to 14 in (35 cm) high and wide; serrated leaves in a rosette close to the ground; yellow flower heads, taproot.	Whether dandelions enhance or disfigure a lawn is a matter of viewpoint. To remove them, dig out the long taproot with the tip of the trowel or an asparagus knife.

Interesting Information

▶ Many building lots were originally farm fields or meadows. Therefore the soil harbors countless weed seeds, which germinate again and again, to the annoyance of the gardener. Remove all seedlings before they form new seeds.

▶ As much as possible, avoid using any chemical weed killers!

▶ To be environmentally safe, remove weeds between pathway stones with a torch (rent from a commercial supplier).

Working and Improving the Soil

Information in Brief

Soil Testing

Dissolve the soil sample in some water (see illustration below).
Test the pH value of your soil with a testing stick, which you can buy. Follow the manufacturer's directions.

Tools

Spade
Spading fork

Materials for Soil Improvement

Humus for sandy and clay soils
Straw with manure for clay soils
Sand for clay soils
Stone or clay meal for sandy soils

Time Expenditure

Digging and working materials in:
About 30 minutes for every 2 yd² (m²)
Loosening the soil:
5–10 minutes for every 2 yd² (m²)

Sandy Soil

Sand cannot be formed into a shape at all. Dry sandy soil is fine and pours through your fingers. Sand is well aerated, water-permeable, and can be easily worked. Sandy soils contain very few nutrients and, in particular, they do not retain any fertilizers that may be added.

Humusy Soil

Humus or compost is not a soil type in the garden. But you can achieve compost-rich soil through regular applications of compost. Humus dissolved in water is black.

Loamy Soil

Loam can be formed into little balls that are not stable, however, and crumble with slight pressure (see bottom left). Loamy soils are among the most fertile soils. They usually have a humus element, hold water, and are well aerated. Loam dissolved in water colors the water above it ochre.

From left to right: sand, humus, loam

Before planting your garden, you must check the quality of the soil and make improvements if necessary.

Soil Improvement

Don't try to "improve" all the garden soil at once but take it bed by bed. First dig the area down with the spade about 12 in (30 cm). Put in the materials for soil improvement. Break up the clods with the spading fork and mix in the appropriate materials step by step. Pull the cultivator or garden rake through the bed to loosen the soil and prepare for planting.

Loosening Soil

The soil between plants in perennial beds has to be loosened. In spring, incorporate compost and organic fertilizer into the bed. Use a cultivator or rake to carefully work the materials into the bed, being careful not to injure the roots of perennials. Finally, cover the surface with mulch. In the summer it will then be enough to occasionally loosen the soil between plants.

Mulching

A 1–3-in (2–7 cm) layer of mulch of shredded bark pieces, leaf mold, or cut grass (mixed with compost) suppresses weed growth and keeps the soil from drying out. You can also sow green fertilizer or cover plants until the next planting. Cover plants such as, clover, lupine, and vetch live in symbiosis with soil bacteria that turn nitrogen from the air into mineral nitrogren. Thus soil erosion is prevented, fertility is increased, and as the cover crops' roots grow and loosen the soil, good soil aeration is provided.

EXPERT TIP
Use grass cuttings for mulch.

Establishing a New Bed

Information in Brief

Materials

Compost
Material for soil
improvement

Tools

2 Stakes
String
Spade
Spading fork
Cultivator or garden rake

Time Expenditure

For a 6 × 6 ft (2 × 2 m) bed:
about 3–4 hours

Putting in Curbing

1. Dig a trench
   (stone depth plus 2–4
   in [5–10 cm])
2. Fill with 1 part cement
   plus 5 parts sand and
   pebbles (lean concrete)
3. Press in stones
4. Fill in edge with lean
   concrete
5. Water
6. Let harden for a few days

Establishing the Outlines of the Bed

First draw the location, size, and shape of the planned bed on a garden plan. Beds with straight edges have a stronger effect than round or curving beds. Isolated island beds in the lawn have a stronger visual effect, because of the "green frame," than beds around the perimeter and thus need greater attention to planting and maintenance.

Transferring the Bed Shape into the Garden

Transfer the bed you have designed on the plan to your garden: For rectangular beds, mark the corner points with bamboo stakes and stretch a string around the bed-to-be. Beds describing circular arcs are marked out on the surface with a string compass (two stakes joined by a string the length of the radius) and the line of the circle marked with sand. A garden hose is also useful to lay out the shape of a new bed or border. Now go sit down and look at the bed. Is it the way you imagined it?

**Begin the practical work only when
you are certain about the type,
size, and shape of the bed.**

Preparing the Bed

Mark the border line with the spade (cut the edge clean and deep), and dig out the soil. Take a soil sample and improve soil as needed.

Cutting Out Turf

Grass sod is cut with a spade, shallowly, an inch or two (a few centimeters) under the turf. The sod—chopped up somewhat—is placed in the compost pile.

Finishing the Bed

Break up the clods of earth with the spade or the spading fork and smooth the surface with the cultivator or garden rake. Add enough compost to raise the bed to the same level as the lawn. Consider how you want to define the garden-lawn boundary. An open transition looks very natural, but the grass easily invades the border and must be cut out regularly. A firm boundary makes maintenance easier but is more expensive and time-consuming.

Dividing the Bed for Planting

Groupings of a few similar plants usually work better than a random mixture of varying colors and shapes. Spread sand to mark the borders of the planted surface (not too geometrically regular). Estimate the number of plants necessary by using the diameters of plants provided in the Choosing Plants section.

EXPERT TIP
Broadly curving beds look more spacious.

CROSS-REFERENCES
Choosing plants pages 78–145
Painting with flowers pages 148–159

Renovating an Old Bed

Information in Brief

Tools

>   Spading fork
>   Cultivator or garden rake
>   Trowel
>   Tree saw
>   Loppers

Material

>   Humus, compost
>   Organic fertilizer
>   Materials for soil
>   improvement

Time Expenditure

>   About 3–4 hours

When Is the Work Carried Out?

>   Best done in spring

Preparation

In case of doubt about doing over a bed, proceed in steps:

First remove only what you definitely don't like and leave the rest for later. This border is dominated by a large bush, which blocks the view of the perennials. Besides, the weeds have spread everywhere.

Removing Shrubs

Cut the shrub back to a hand's breadth above the soil. The remainder serves as a "handle" for pulling out the shrub. Poke the spading fork under the shrub all around it and lift up the rootstock. Now try to pull the shrub out. If it still won't come out, poke and loosen some of the soil around the bush and then pull again.

Either pull out the weeds or dig them out with the spading fork.

**There are many reasons to do
over a bed: You want to change it,
enlarge it, or redesign it entirely.**

Dividing Perennials
Insert the spading fork all around
the perennial and lift the rootstock
out of the ground. If you want to
reuse the perennial, divide the root
and lay the plants aside, covered
with soil, until you are ready to
replant them.

The Renovated Bed
Do a soil test and improve the soil if
necessary. Fill in any unevenness
with composted soil, which is worked
into the existing soil with a spading
fork. Finally, since the overgrown
plants have removed nutrients from
the soil, spread an organic fertilizer
over the soil and work it in with the
cultivator.

Now plant the open areas with
divided plants and any newly
purchased plants.

Since the disturbing shrub is
gone, the eye now travels up a
bed that rise in stages, grandstand-
like, whose plants flow together in
ribbons of color (from front to back:
yellow evening primroses, yellow
needle-leaved coreopsis, blue sage,
red centranthus, light-blue larkspur).

Should you no longer like the bed
in this form in subsequent years, you
can scale the "ribbons" further by
colorfully matching in plants that are
even taller.

EXPERT TIP
*Put the waste plants on the
compost heap.*

CROSS-REFERENCES
Dividing perennials pages 66–67
Improving the soil pages 26–27

Composting

Information in Brief

Compostable Materials

Garden waste (except for
diseased plant parts!)
Raw kitchen waste
Mulch
Dried grass cuttings
Leaves
Hedge clippings
Straw
Wood ashes
Cardboard (in moderation)
Coffee filters (in moderation)

Noncompostable Materials

Pressure-treated wood
Citrus fruit (sprayed)
Seed-bearing weeds
Weed roots
Meat waste (no bones, either)
Dairy products
Cooked kitchen waste

Tools

Spading fork
Compost sieve

When to Move?

Spring or fall

What Is a Compost Heap?

In composting, the organic material that is created in the house and garden is broken down into its component parts and turned into humus. Humus only develops with the help of soil organisms. Thus it is also necessary for you to provide a connection to living soil (moving), so that bacteria, fungi, worms, beetles, and other small organisms can enter. The breakdown of "garbage" in the compost heap occurs through digestion by these organisms. Make sure the compost is well aerated by adding coarse material (chopped branches, etc.), and on hot summer days treat it to a watering can of water. When air is closed off—for instance, inside a densely packed layer of green grass cuttings—putrefactive bacteria develop. These have no business in compost. You can recognize successful digestion when the compost heap collapses in on itself.

Thermocomposter

With a compost heap you can transform organic wastes from the garden and kitchen into nutrient-rich humus.

Moving Compost
Repile the compost after 2–3 months in a second silo using two hands-breadths of coarse material, alternating with a layer of raw humus and a 2-in (5-cm) -thick layer of garden soil or compost, some organic fertilizer and rock phosphate, possibly also compost starter. Place a layer of garden soil on top.

Mature Compost
In a mature compost heap the earth-worms are active; they regularly eat through the heap and create dark, woodsy-smelling humus. Now you must have patience for 2–3 more months, and then you may "harvest" the finished compost.

Since the mature compost remains undisturbed, you can plant it with nasturtiums, sweet peas, pumpkins, or cucumbers.

Filtering Compost
After the end of the maturing process there are always large chunks left in the mass, and these should not be spread. Therefore the compost should be filtered before it is used.

Working Compost In
You can now store the filtered compost between seasons or spread it on the beds. Put it on the soil in layers about 1/2 in (1 cm) thick, and carefully work it in with a cultivator, hoe, or rake.

EXPERT TIP
Cover the compost heap in heavy rain.

Planting Plants

Planting annuals, perennials, trees, shrubs, or roses is one of the nicest and most satisfying jobs in the garden year.

Carefully consider which and how many trees, shrubs, and perennials you want to put in your garden, and determine whether the plants that have caught your eye are suitable for the chosen location. In any case, take enough time for the preparations. Using the portraits and design sections, make your choices ahead of time, and only then put together a shopping list.

If you have to start the garden from the very beginning, it's best to plan in stages. Still, you should enjoy your garden all year long; care in choosing will more than repay you afterward. Particularly with woody plants, careful planning pays. Do you want to put in a single-row hedge and build a uniform green wall, or do you prefer a staggered shrub border, which livens up the garden and also offers privacy in summer?

Trees are wonderful woody plants, but they become large, and their shadows can inhibit the growth of other plants. Does it necessarily have to be a mighty tree, though? A beautiful shrub tree, for instance a Japanese maple or a small-crowned fruit tree, offers both height and an attractive focal point that fits into a small garden well without overwhelming it. Also, various green-clad frames of ramblers or climbers provide points of interest, serve as privacy screens, or create rooms.

When to Plant?

The best time for planting is on a cloudy day or on a day that is not very sunny or hot.

▶ In spring, nursery inventories are especially abundant; this is the time to plant perennials and perhaps hardy annuals.

▶ Trees, shrubs, and roses with bare roots are planted in the fall. The fall is also the planting time for bulbs and corms that are to bloom the following spring.

▶ Lawns can be sown throughout the entire growing season.

Anyone with only a small space for planting can resort to using various containers.

Plant Choices and Buying

When buying plants there are some important things you should keep in mind:

▶ Bulbs, corms, and tubers are usually sold in perforated plastic bags, and you find all the necessary directions on the attached label. The bulbs or corms must not have any dark or moldy spots. They must feel firm and springy—not soft—and must not yet have begun to sprout (green leaf tips are visible).

▶ Annuals and biennials are either grown from seed by oneself or bought as started plants. These can turn beds into blooming areas very quickly.

▶ Perennials should be compact and bushy. "Straggly" (or leggy) plants with long, leafless areas of stem will not usually recover again. The leaves should be a strong green. Spots may indicate disease. Light-green to yellow spots indicate nutrient deficiencies. If the roots are growing through the bottom hole or out of splits in the side of the container, it is better to choose another plant, for this one is rootbound, that is, it has been in the container too long.

▶ Trees and shrubs are perennial woody plants. Since you receive them in budding condition, the sale is a matter of trust. Therefore go to a reputable nursery and get detailed advice.

The Available Forms

Trees, shrubs, and perennials are available in different forms.

▶ Perennials, small shrubs, and trees today are offered almost without exception in plastic containers. You must pay attention to the rootstock of shrubs and small trees. Pull carefully on the trunk: If the entire ball can be pulled out and the roots are growing around it and are dense and intertwined, it is better to choose another specimen. Container plants can be planted all year round. These plants can also be left for a few days in their containers—watered but not forgotten—without any harm being done.

▶ Plastic pots and flats are typical containers for annuals and biennials.

▶ Large perennials, shrubs, or roses are sometimes wrapped in black

Worth the Money—Your Own Seedlings

Growing flowers or vegetables from seed is economical but is not always easy to do and is a relatively time-consuming business.

plastic. Plants packed in this way can be handled like container plants.

▶ Trees and shrubs (including roses) are offered balled or bare root.

▶ With balled plants, the tree or shrub is lifted from a bed and the roots, together with soil, are wrapped in burlap or plastic. They should still be covered with soil in the nursery, or else they will dry out. If you have to store the plant for a while after you've bought it and before you plant it, make sure it is watered and place it in a lightly shaded area if possible.

▶ Woody plants with bare roots are only sold during the plant's dormant phase (fall to early spring). They may only be kept for a short time—lying in a trench and covered with soil.

To Sow Flower Seeds or Not?

Sowing seeds is the least expensive way to fill your summer beds with a glory of color. Dealing with seeds is not difficult, but particularly for the beginner, extra care is needed especially if you have poor garden soil. The directions on the seed packets sound very simple, but if after sowing, not one of the promised plants appears, perhaps you may need to improve your soil by adding more filtered compost, breaking up large soil clods, and making sure seeds did not dry out. The most certain—but labor-intensive—approach is starting seeds indoors.

Garden centers and nurseries offer abundant choices of plants almost all year long.

▶ Use a container about 3 in (8 cm) in depth and a seed-starting soil mix.

▶ Make a groove in the soil with a little stick and sow the seeds (according to package directions). Carefully water in seeds. Cover with clear plastic to keep moisture level high.

▶ Let the container stand at room temperature (70–75°F [21–24°C]) (not on a heating unit!) until the first green appears. Keep soil moist. Do not allow it to dry out. Make sure seedlings get at least 14–16 hours of light each day.

▶ Pick out the strongest plants with a transplanting stick (a flat piece of wood works too)—and put each in a little pot. Fertilize with a dilute solution after seedlings are a few inches in height.

▶ When they are sturdy enough, plant them directly in the bed.

EXPERT TIP
Don't let the plants you've bought stand in the sun.

Seeding Lawns

Information in Brief

Tools

  Spade or spading fork
  Metal rake
  Roller (rented) or stepping
  boards
  Seed spreader (later use to
  spread fertilizer)
  Lawn sprinkler or garden
  hose
  String and stakes
  Spirit level

Materials

  Seed (lawn mixture)
  Sand
  Humus or topsoil
  Complete fertilizer (containing
  potassium and magnesium)

Time Expenditure

Seeding (spreader) and rolling:
    about 5 minutes per 11
    square feet (square meter)
Seeding (hand) and tamping
down:
    about 30 minutes per 11
    square feet (square meter)

Preparing the Soil

Break up the lawn-to-be with the spade or spading fork and remove large stones, construction trash, sticks, and roots, or water puddles may develop later. Lawns need light soil, so undertake improvement measures by adding organic matter and a complete fertilizer ahead of time.

Stretch out squares with string (about 15 × 15 ft [5 × 5 m]), and level the ground in each square with the rake again and again (use a spirit level). The land should fall slightly away from the house, otherwise rainwater will run toward the house.

Preparing the Soil for Seeding

Sprinkle a soil-sand mixture on the prepared surface that can be enriched by additional rock phosphate. The ideal lawn soil is loose. Scratch it into the upper soil layer gently with the rake. Wait 2–3 weeks until any possible weed seeds present have sprouted and the soil has settled. Compress the soil with a heavy roller or stamp the surface flat using stamping boards under your shoes and pressing hard.

Tell the clerk at the garden center how you plan to use your lawn, and then buy the seed mixture recommended for that purpose.

Seeding the Lawn

Grass seed is sold by the square foot (square meter), so measure the surface. A little before seeding, loosen the soil crosswise with a rake (don't press down). A seed spreader distributes the seed evenly. Mix the grass seed with some sand and pull the spreader over the ground in swaths. Sowing by hand is far more difficult. Divide the surface area and spread the seed as evenly as possible.

Rolling

After seeding, the seed is worked into the ground. First draw the rake over the surface without applying any pressure. Rent a roller and roll it over the grass.

Tamping Firm

An alternative to rolling is homemade stamping boards (boards with strings or leather straps for the feet). Use these to press the seed in step by step. Tamp down flat so that no ridges occur.

Watering

Besides warmth, your lawn now needs a great deal of consistent watering. Use a sprinkler, or spray with a fine spray from the hose. The stream of water should not hit the ground hard or the seed will be washed to one side and the lawn will sprout irregularly.

You must water daily until the first green shows. Only when the new lawn is 2–3 in (5–8 cm) high can it be mowed for the first time to a height of about 1 in (3 cm). Now add lawn fertilizer to the irrigation water (follow directions on the package).

EXPERT TIP
Build a tree well into your plans for a tree.

CROSS-REFERENCE
Improving the soil pages 26–27

Installing Turf

Information in Brief

Tools

Wheelbarrow
Board
Roller (rental) or tamping boards
Lawn sprinkler or garden hose
String and stakes
Spirit level

Materials

Turf rolls
Sand
Humus or topsoil
Complete fertilizer (containing potassium and magnesium)

Time Expenditure

Laying:
5–10 minutes per 11 sq ft (m²)

When to Do It

Preferably from August to September, but also possible throughout the growing season.

Turf

Many garden centers offer turf in the form of rolls or squares. This spares you the somewhat tricky work of seeding. However, grass in this form is obviously more expensive than grass seed. Rolls of turf are somewhat sturdier than individual blocks.

Consider the purpose you want it for and buy the type of grass accordingly.

Laying Turf

Using the spirit level and the rake, create a level soil surface. Begin rolling out the turf along a straight edge. When the first strip is rolled out, put a board across it so as not to injure the freshly laid grass by walking on it. Repeat the procedure for the second and succeeding strips.

Grass is not just grass.

If you think it is important to have an "instant lawn," which will make your yard green immediately, you should choose pregrown turf or sod.

Cutting Edges

Tamp the grass down with a roller or with stamping boards. Now use an edging tool or a spade to cut the edges. Use a stretched string as a marking line for straight edges.

Making Contours

Round or scalloped edges are marked with a string compass, sprinkled with sand, and cut with the edging tool. Or use something like a sharp knife as the movable part of the "compass" to cut the edges.

Laying Turf Blocks

Make an even surface to receive the sod. Turf blocks are not laid in an even row but are staggered. Use as wide a board for walking as possible so as not to injure the freshly laid turf.

The edges are done the same way as with rolled turf.

Watering

Both rolled and block turf must be carefully raked with a bamboo rake after being laid in order to remove any loose remnants. Then, water thoroughly. Turf lawns can be walked on carefully after a few days, but they are not suitable for play or for being walked on by a number of people for 3–4 weeks.

EXPERT TIP
Install pregrown turf at once.

CROSS-REFERENCES
Soil preparation pages 39–40
String compass pages 28–29

Planting Perennials

Information in Brief

Materials

Trowel
Hand cultivator
Bucket of water
Watering can
Humus
Materials for soil
improvement

Planting Time

Container plants can be
planted any time of year,
but spring is the best time.
Plant on a dull day without
strong sun.

Time Expenditure

5–10 minutes per plant

Preparing the Planting Hole
Begin planting in the center of the
bed and work out to the edges. Dig a
hole with the trowel about the size
of the root ball, plus a few inches
around the edge. Loosen the bottom
and sides of the planting hole with
the hand cultivator. With very heavy
or light soils it's a good idea to
"improve" around the area of the
planting hole.

Putting in the Plant
Place the planting container in a
bucket of water for about 20 minutes
so that the roots are thoroughly
moistened. Pull off the plastic pot
and loosen the tangled roots. The
roots should be pulled free at the
sides and bottom so that they can be
easily spread out. Then put the root
ball in the planting hole. The upper
edges of the ball must be level with
the ground. Correct the depth by
digging deeper or filling in with soil.

Long-lived perennials stamp the character of a garden to a considerable degree. They should complement one another in color and growth form.

Spreading the Roots

Carefully spread out the roots in the planting hole and make sure that the upper surface of the ball is roughly horizontal. Put a little water in the planting hole so that the edges and bottom are well moistened.

Filling In with Soil

Using a trowel, mix the soil removed in digging with some humus, and fill in around the root ball with the mixture. Water a little more, so that the soil particles wash in among the roots, enclose them firmly, and support them.

Now completely fill in the hole with soil. Use your knuckles to press the soil firmly down around the new plant. Now add some more of the humus-garden soil mixture and smooth the bed surface.

Watering In

Now the new plant should be watered thoroughly to provide the roots with sufficient water—transplanting is stressful for the plant! Watering also helps settle soil particles in between the roots, which compresses large air pockets in the soil. Remember to water regularly during the days that follow, but do not overwater.

EXPERT TIP
Annuals and biennials are planted like perennials.

CROSS-REFERENCES
Soil improvement pages 26–27
Choosing plants pages 78–145

Planting Bulbs, Corms, and Tubers

Information in Brief

Materials

Dibble
Bulb planter
Watering can
Plastic basket

Planting Time

Spring flowers in fall
Fall flowers in spring

Time Expenditure

1–2 minutes per bulb or corm

Colorful Spring Plantings

Bulbs and corms come into their own in spring—they provide the first color in the garden. Arrange the plants you buy in the fall in natural looking groups so that several similar plants are next to each other. Use this trick to avoid a too-regular arrangement: Let the small bulbs and corms fall from your hand onto the ground and put them in where they fall. With larger bulbs use a substitute like pebbles or game tiles. After they flower, cut only the blooms off; the foliage can be cut off just at the ground after they wither.

While perennials are immediately visible after planting, bulbs, corms, and tubers only appear after a resting phase.

Planting in a Basket

Naturally you can simply leave the bulbs, corms, and tubers in the ground until the next year, but it's better to dry them over the winter and store them in a cool place. If the bulbs are planted in a basket, they are easier to take up again.

Dahlia Tubers

Dahlias are planted in the spring and must be removed from the garden before the first frost. Let the removed tubers dry out; shake off the soil and store them in a cool, dark place.

Bulbs

There are special hollow bulb planters (big holes) for bulbs and corms and dibbles (small holes), which make the work much easier. Look carefully at the bulbs. The root side must be down, the sprouting side up (usually the pointed end). If you are unsure, ask when you buy them. Put the bulb or corm in the hole, fill it with soil, and water it.

A "Wild" Meadow

Crocus, grape hyacinths, small narcissi, and species tulips lend a natural wild charm to a field area. Scatter the corms or bulbs in the grass in the fall. Use the spade to make cuts under the sod and put the tubers or corms and bulbs in. Afterwards replace the sod in its original spot.

The flowers appear in the spring along with the growing grass. Wait to mow the lawn until the leaves of the bulbs and corms have withered.

EXPERT TIP
Mark the planting spots with a stake.

CROSS-REFERENCES
Spring flowers pages 82–91
Lawn care pages 62–65

Planting Shrubs

Information in Brief

Forms Offered

Container shrubs
Balled shrubs
Bare-root shrubs

Tools

Spading fork and spade
Sledgehammer (support)
Watering can

Materials

Garden twine, jute, or tree tape
Supporting stake
Humus
Horn or bone meal

Planting Time

Spring to fall
Container plants all seasons

Time Expenditure

1–2 hours per shrub

Watering

If you can't plant the shrub soon after you buy it, it can be heeled in, the roots covered with soil, in the garden until you can deal with it. At least an hour before planting, place the shrub in a bucket of water so that the roots become saturated. With burlap-balled shrubs, leave the cloth on the ball.

The Planting Hole

With the spading fork or spade dig a hole that is about as deep and twice as wide as the ball, and loosen the soil in the bottom to a depth of about 20 in (50 cm). Loosen the soil at the sides of the hole with the spading fork.

Put in the Shrub

Check the depth of the hole. The shrub must be planted at the same depth as it was at the nursery. Then put in the plant; with balled plants, plastic wrap is now carefully removed. Burlap can be kept around the root ball as long as some slits are made around the balled area.

When you are planting shrubs, bear in mind the shrub's mature height and spread. Every shrub needs adequate space to spread out.

Filling In the Soil

Mix the soil removed from the planting hole with some humus, so that the shrub will develop roots more easily. With nutrient-poor soil, add some horn or bone meal. Fill the amended soil back in around the plant. Bare-root plants are very carefully rocked back and forth so that the earth sifts in around the roots and the shrub rests more securely. Press the earth down with your fist and then with your feet, being careful not to press too hard and injure the roots. With the remaining soil, form a crater around the planting hole (firm by lightly tamping around the outside).

Watering and Staking

Fill the crater with water from the watering can or hose and repeat this procedure several times until the soil is thoroughly moistened. Wide-spreading shrubs need not be staked. Narrow shrubs exposed to strong winds should be protected with a stake on the wind side (fastened to a main shoot with garden twine).

Cutting Back

Sometimes because of the reduction of root mass (bare roots, cutting off the ball) cutting back some of the above-ground parts is necessary. Ask about this when you are buying plants and ask a nursery worker to do this pruning for you if you are going to be planting the shrub immediately afterward. Otherwise cut the shrub back to the sturdiest main shoots; new side growth will come out of these.

EXPERT TIP
Have large shrubs delivered.

CROSS-REFERENCES
Soil improvement pages 26–27
Pruning shrubs pages 66–67

Planting Roses

Information in Brief

Available Forms

Container roses
Bare-root roses

Tools

Spade or spading fork
Trowel
Pruning shears
Watering can
Gloves

Materials

Humus or compost
Horn and bone meal and
rock phosphate

Planting Time

Late fall or spring
Container plants all seasons

Time Expenditure

Preparation:
2–3 weeks for soil
improvement
2–12 hours soaking
Planting:
about 30 minutes per rose

Preparation of Soil and Soaking

Three to 4 weeks before planting, dig a planting hole 2 spade-lengths deep, and mix the removed soil with a bucketful of humus or compost, horn and bone meal, and rock phosphate. Then put it all back in the planting hole.

Bare-root roses must never be allowed to dry out, and thus, immediately after buying should be immersed in a bucket of water (leave for 3–12 hours). This is even more important if you order roses from a catalog and receive them by mail or parcel delivery.

Root Pruning

This step is not necessary with container roses. A rose has at least two or three green canes, roots, and in the middle of these the so-called bud union. It is at this point that a short scion piece with a bud has been grafted onto the rootstock of a wild rose, out of which the hybrid tea rose will grow. Prune away any injured (broken or bent) root sections and shorten the other roots to about 6–8 in (15–20 cm) in length. Finally, dip the roots in a slurry of loam and water to coat them.

Roses need deep, nutrient-rich soil in a sunny location with good air circulation.

Planting

Dig a hole in the prepared soil with the spade or trowel. It must be double the size of the plant and deep enough so that entire root system will fit in without cramping and the bud union will be about a handsbreadth (2–4 in [5–10 cm]) under the surface of the soil (make trial placements).

Filling in the Soil

Mix the removed soil with humus or compost and fill in around the roots. Wiggle the rose gently back and forth so that the earth settles down between the roots. Keep adding a little water.

Watering In

Pile the soil into a heap 6–8 in (15–20 cm) high around the bud union ("hilling"). When roses are planted in the fall, this hill is left there for the entire winter. Water well with a watering can so there are no hollow areas in the soil. Repeat this procedure several times until the soil is thoroughly wet.

Roses planted in the spring soon put out new growth; remove the hilled soil after 3–4 weeks (wear gloves!).

Pruning

Container roses are not pruned after planting; wait until the following spring. Fall-planted roses with bare roots should be shortened to a manageable 12–16 in (30–40 cm) (but this is usually done by the nursery); also leave the final pruning until spring in this case.

Roses planted in spring are pruned back to about 4–5 eyes (buds) on strong canes, to about 2–4 eyes on thin canes.

EXPERT TIP
Buy roses from a specialty nursery.

CROSS-REFERENCES
Pruning roses pages 74–75
Choosing plants pages 134–139

Planting a Hedge

Information in Brief

Forms Available

Container shrubs
Balled shrubs
Bare-root shrubs

Tools

Spading fork or spade
Watering can or hose

Materials

Humus
Horn or bone meal

Planting Time

Fall to spring
Container plants all seasons

Time Expenditure

1–2 hours per yard (meter)
of hedge

Preparation
Measure the length of the planned hedge and have the nursery advise you how many hedge shrubs must be planted at what interval. Stretch a string along the ground where the hedge is to be planted and dig planting holes, or for closely planted shrubs (e.g., privet, hornbeam) a trench. Loosen the soil down to 20 in (50 cm).

Planting Shrubs
If you have poor soil, mix compost and horn or bone meal in with the removed soil. Put the shrub in exactly on the hedge line. With loose hedges, proceed from plant hole to plant hole; with dense hedges, place the shrubs next to one another in the trench. If the shrubs were sold with twine or wire around them, leave them tied up until time to prune— you can handle them more easily if the branches are tied up.

Open hedges of staggered shrubs need more space, but they are less labor-intensive than clipped hedges.

Filling in the Soil

Now fill in the hole or trench with the amended soil. Correct the placement of the shrubs: They should be straight and the same distance from one another (for clipped hedges). Tamp down the soil carefully with your feet, and then form an earth wall around the shrub.

Irrigation

Settle the loose soil particles down around the roots with plenty of water. For longer hedges it is a good idea to use a garden hose to thoroughly water in the plants.

Also water thoroughly in the days that follow.

Now open up any bound up branches so that they can hang out before you prune.

Pruning

If the nursery has not done it, you must now cut back the main shoot of deciduous shrubs about a third of their length and shorten side shoots by about half. Evergreens are not pruned; they must reach their full height first.

EXPERT TIP
Discuss planting a hedge with your neighbor first.

CROSS-REFERENCES
Planting shrubs pages 46–47
Choosing plants pages 122–123

Planting Trees

Information in Brief

Forms Available

Container trees
Balled trees
Bare-root trees

Tools

Spading forks and spades
Sledgehammer (support)
Watering can or hose

Materials

Garden twine, jute, or tree tape
Support stake
Humus
Horn or bone meal

Planting Time

In areas of colder winters
and frost fall to spring
Container plants anytime in
mild climates

Time Expenditure

About 2 hours per tree

Preparation and Tree Planting

For stability and uptake of water and nutrients trees need a voluminous root system. Dig a planting hole (double the breadth of the ball), and loosen the subsoil (to about 32 in [80 cm] deep) as well as the side walls of the hole with the spading fork.

Amend the removed soil with humus and horn and bone meal. Place the tree in the planting hole; it must be situated at exactly the same depth as in the nursery.

Removing the Cloth

Carefully cut the string of the balling cloth with scissors or a knife. Cut the cloth and pull it from the ball in strips. Some remnants of burlap or landscape cloth can remain on the ball, since the roots will grow through it and later the material will rot in the ground. However, if plastic was used to wrap the ball, it must be completely removed from the ball.

Trees form the look of any garden with their prominent shapes. Look for the optimum location before you plant.

Driving Stakes

Drive a stake in the soil of the planting hole next to the ball. Check its stability with a test wiggle. The stake must be set on the side facing the direction of the prevailing winds.

Anchoring the Tree

Wrap tree tape (or strong garden twine/jute) around the trunk, twist it into a figure eight, and tie it loosely to the stake; after one to two weeks tie it firmly. Evergreens are tied to a slanting stake.

Filling in the Soil

Check to see that the tree trunk is vertical; you can still correct it. Fill in the planting hole with the amended soil. If the tree has bare roots, rock the trunk carefully back and forth so that the soil will sift down among the roots. Water at intervals for better distribution of the soil, and keep adding water. Tamp the soil firmly with your feet, and form a small crater with the rest of the removed soil.

Watering

Now water inside the crater and sluice in the fine soil particles between the roots with the watering can or hose; repeat several times after the water has sunk in. Also, water the tree in the days that follow; however, not as much as when sluicing it in.

EXPERT TIP
Check the location with a stand-in.

CROSS-REFERENCES
Staking trees pages 68–69
Pruning branches pages 70–71

Planting Tubs and Boxes

Information in Brief

Tools

Trowel
Watering can

Materials

Potting soil
Clay shards or
Pebbles

Planting Time

All year long, as wanted

Time Expenditure

About 30 minutes for a
medium-sized tub

Planter Forms

Terracotta (natural):
elegant to rustic
Glazed clay:
in numerous styles
Plastic:
lightweight and inexpensive
Wood:
only with inner coating
Metal:
striking

Preparing a Flower Box
Only buy planters with drainage holes in the bottom or water will collect. Put shards of broken clay pots or pebbles in the bottom to cover the holes so water can drain out but soil does not.

Filling with Soil
Now put in potting soil (from the garden center or some sand mixed with compost), deep enough so that the top of the root ball of the largest plants will come up to about 2 in (3 cm) from the top of the planter when you place the plants in the soil. Plants should not be closer than 2 in (3 cm) from all sides. Press the soil down gently.

Containers, which are quickly planted and universally useful, liven up the look of the garden.

Planting the Plants in the Middle
Begin with planting the middle of the box with the largest and tallest plants. Add some potting soil so that the plants stand firm. Fill in enough soil to make the remaining plants come within 2 in (3 cm) of the edge of the box.

Planting the Remaining Plants
Distribute the other plants in the box. When in bloom, all the flowers should be easily visible without the boxes looking too symmetrical. Also plan for trailing plants.

Make sure you have a harmonious picture when you choose the colors of the flowers.

Filling In Soil and Watering
Now fill in between the plants with the rest of the soil. Press it firmly with your fingers. There should be a 2-in (3-cm) watering space between the top of the soil and the edge of the planter. The soil absorbs the seeping water and the excess drains off at the bottom.

Test the soil with your finger on hot days and if necessary, water several times a day since container plantings dry out faster than in-ground plantings.

EXPERT TIP
Several small pots look more lively than one large one.

CROSS-REFERENCE
Painting with flowers pages 148–155

Plant Care

"No pain, no gain," also applies to the garden. Organize well to get the necessary jobs done.

To many people "maintenance" mainly means tiresome work. Since you want the garden to relax in, there appears to be a contradiction here. On the other hand, a poorly maintained garden soon provides little relaxation.

One way out of this dilemma is the choice of a garden type from the start. Those who are sure of their unswerving aversion to garden work, but nevertheless, want some green around them, should go for an "easy–care" garden as much as possible and select plants that are low-maintenance.

Garden Work as Pleasure

Why do we make such a sharp distinction between work and leisure? Obviously because work is necessary but doesn't always satisfy us, so we look for fulfillment in our time off. Gardening can be one of the most satisfying, exciting elements of your free time. Don't think first of the amount of work required but regard it as a leisure-time pleasure. It is a wonderful feeling to step back and regard a cleanly pruned bush. It will put out new growth and reward you all year long with a beautiful growth form, attractive leaves, and splendid flowers.

The same goes for the extremely time-consuming duties of maintaining perennial beds. Don't get upset with the tiresome tasks of weeding, fertilizing, and watering, but think about these jobs in a new positive way. With every hour of work, you get a little closer to your goal—a magnificently flowering bed. If you put off such work or don't do it at all, the vexation over a garden run wild is enormous and saps your free-time pleasure. Don't take on too much at once, instead take small, accomplishable steps.

The required techniques are easy to learn—and they are presented on the pages that follow.

The larger and more varied the garden, the more labor intensive it is. But, it's worth the effort.

Garden Chores

You can regard the care of your garden plants as hard or easy, complicated or simple. Certainly the temperament of the gardener plays a role too. Impulsive people go into the garden on a Saturday afternoon and start working at anything their eye falls on. Systematic people make precise plans and work through them step-by-step. The path to a perfect garden always lies somewhere in between. Specific, regularly occurring jobs are best accomplished according to a plan, while others can be done according to preference—and mood! Each person keeps a professional and/or private appointment calendar, why not one for the garden, too, in which the most important dates are marked?

Annual Jobs

Plan ahead for the long term, for such jobs always require a certain amount of time.

▶ Once a year the compost heap has to be moved and the compost spread on beds. So reserve a day for it in early spring; plants putting out new growth are especially grateful for it then.

▶ Also the pruning of trees and shrubs demands care, and with it a certain expenditure of time. There is no point in putting off this job for too long—you should try to be finished by the beginning of the growing season at the latest.

▶ If perennials are overgrown, they are best divided in early spring or after flowering in late summer or early fall. The fall is not too late to divide perennials since perennials will form new roots up until the very beginning of winter. Therefore, you will be giving them a jump start for spring.

Seasonal Jobs

Foremost among these is fertilizing. Since it is scarcely possible to give any absolute rules for fertilizing, details about fertilization requirements are provided in the plant portraits.

▶ Make a checklist on which you note the fertilizing time for a particular plant and can cross it off so you know it has been done.

Once a year you should provide the soil with a slow-release administration of organic fertilizer (e.g., horn chips or bone meal) according to the manufacturer's instructions.

▶ Several times a year the mulch on the beds should be renewed, too. Grass clippings should be saved for the compost. Spread the clippings or composted weeds on the beds. They make a good summer mulch. The ground stays moist and heavy rainstorms don't fall directly on the soil and cause erosion problems.

In the fall collected leaves can be spread under bushes and trees. Water leaves a bit so they don't blow away.

The fine bark mulch offered commercially breaks down very slowly. In fall it should be applied in a thin layer, and in spring in a mixture with humus on the beds. Also berry bushes and hedges are very grateful for an application of bark mulch in spring and fall.

▶ If you have a large garden with numerous trees and shrubs, a large number of branches fall regularly. Only in such cases does it pay to get a chipper-shredder to produce material for mulch and compost.

Safety Must Still Come First
Use safety glasses and wear gloves when chipping and shredding.

Watering is one of the most time-consuming garden chores— a sprinkler helps save time.

Jobs That Need to Be Done Often

Everyone knows that a lawn should be mowed about once a week.

▶ However, it is just as important, especially in spring, that the beds be weeded regularly so that weeds can't get established. Always remove weeds before they flower so they have no chance to spread further. Perennial weeds like goutweed and bindweed (see pages 24–25) are very difficult to eradicate—and only if you stay after them constantly and carefully remove every little rootlet.

▶ During the chief blooming season go through the garden with scissors every day for 10 minutes and cut off any spent flowers. This is much more than a "cosmetic" measure, for it will help stimulate plants to produce a second generation of flowers out of side buds.

▶ Don't forget watering. You can water individual plants with a watering can, but for larger lawns or borders it pays to use a watering system (sprinkler or perforated hose).

Set up sprinklers, turn on water, and you're done. Water in the morning or the evening, never during the day in the sunshine. To make sure watering is even easier and consistent, add a simple timing device to your system.

Recognizing and Treating Plant Injury

How the Injury Looks	Description	Treatment and Tips

Aphids on Roses
Green to almost-black little aphids collect on the fresh, green plant parts (roses and other plants); leaves roll up, become wavy, buds wilt.

Aphids are the food for many beneficial insects such as ladybugs; therefore only use chemical preparations with heavy infestations. Add 1 to 2 tablespoons of dish-washing soap to a spray bottle to control aphids. Can also use yellow sticky traps.

Roseslugs
Insect is only 0.2 in (5 mm) long; it lays its eggs under rose leaves; the 0.4-in (1-cm) -long larva eats window-like holes in the leaves.

Serious damage only occurs with repeated, massive attacks. Then use a contact insecticide (from garden center or dealer).

Powdery Mildew
Fungus that invades from spores through the openings in the leaves (roses, vegetables, berries, perennials); whitish deposit on the leaves.

Prevent by not wetting the leaves when watering and keeping enough distance between plants. Rotate plantings. Pull out infected plants to avoid spreading spores. Remove plant waste in the fall from plant-ings. Only use fungicide (garden center) in the case of severe attack.

Downy Mildew
Fungus disease on vegetables and grapes; undersides of leaves with whitish gray spots, upper sides with yellow to reddish-brown spots.

Treat like powdery mildew.

No one is immune to insects, fungus, and plant viruses. But don't reach for the "chemical club" for every disease. Also, consult with your local cooperative extension agency for the best organic and safe chemical prevention and control strategies.

How the Injury Looks	Description	Treatment and Tips
	**Scab** Fungus disease of fruit trees (apple, pear); at first olive-green dark spots on the leaves, then dark spots and scars on the fruit.	Prevention: Sufficient distance between plants, light crowns. Ask when buying fruit trees for resistant varieties. Only use fungicide (garden center) with heavy infection.
	**Monilia Disease (Brown Rot)** Mold on stone fruits and cherries. Injuries are required for infection. Rings of circularly developing mold.	Remove the fruit at the first sign of attack. Plant disease-resistant varieties.
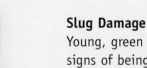	**Fire Blight** Rare bacterial disease in stone fruit and some ornamental shrubs. The buds become black and do not put out new growth. The branches look burned.	Immediately and extensively prune back branches showing the first symptoms and burn them; under no circumstances put in the compost! Disinfect pruning shears between cuts and after using.
	Slug Damage Young, green shoots with clear signs of being eaten. Slugs are nocturnal and hide during the day.	It's best to collect slugs; set up slug fences or slug traps; cover valuable plants at night with a Mason jar. Spread eggshells or sharp pieces of gravel around plants.

Lawn Mowing, Watering, and Fertilizing

Information in Brief

Cutting Height for Grass

Working lawns (ones to be walked on and used):
> 1¹/₄–2 in (30–50 mm) in spring, fall, and in extreme drought
> 1 in (25 mm) in summer

Ornamental lawn (rarely walked on):
> 1 in (25 mm) in spring, fall, and extreme drought
> ¹/₂–1 in (12–25 mm) in summer

Tools

> **Mower with basket and adjustable cutting heights**
> **Grass trimmer**
> **Edger**
> **Fertilizer spreader**
> **Sprinkler or hose**

Time Expenditure

Watering:
> About 20 minutes for each area sprinkled

Fertilizing:
> With the fertilizer cart, 5 minutes per 11 square feet

Mowing Lawns

Grasses have a dense root system—they need water, nutrients, and must be mowed regularly. First mow the edge of the grass area, and then mow strip by strip, slightly overlapping, over the entire lawn. Mow when the grass is about 1 inch above its recommended height. Cutting it too short adversely affects root development and the ability of the plant to manufacture food.

Ornamental lawns must be mowed more often than working lawns.

Mowing with the Grass Trimmer

In steeply sloping areas, on very irregular ground, large "wild meadows," or between dense stands of trees, it is easier mowing with a grass trimmer (string cutter). This electrical tool (cable or battery) cuts the blades of grass with a rotating plastic string. The cuttings are left where they fall and must be removed with a rake.

For safety reasons, wear sturdy shoes or rubber boots when mowing with the grass trimmer.

The lawn is the yard's "showpiece." To keep it that way, it must be regularly and carefully maintained.

Mowing Problem Areas

Wherever the normal lawn mowers can't go, cut the grass with a hand clipper or an electric edger. At the edges of lawns, along paved walks, in front of walls, or in close corners, you must resort to this labor-intensive method. Some edge cutters have a long handle so that this work doesn't have to be performed on your knees.

Fertilizing

Lawn fertilizers are usually sold in the form of granules. Scatter the fertilizer in midspring with a spreader or evenly by hand after first mowing the lawn. Follow the directions on the fertilizer package. Then set up the sprinkler and water it in (unless the weather report predicts rain!). The water dissolves the fertilizer granules and washes the fertilizer down to the root area. Undissolved fertilizer burns the grass and causes unattractive yellowish brown spots in the full green, so take care to follow the manufacturer's directions and not overfertilize.

Watering

Don't spare the water during hot summers (at least once a week in the evening)—your lawn will thank you. Automatic impulse sprinklers (large areas) distribute the water in segments of circles, circular sprinklers (small areas) in whole, size-adjustable circles, and rectangular sprinklers rectangularly. In small areas the hose with a fine spray will also do (time-consuming). A good rule of thumb is to provide 1 in (2 cm) of water to the lawn and garden each week. This means leaving a sprinkler system on for about one hour each week if there has not been adequate natural rainfall.

EXPERT TIP
In summer mow about once a week.

CROSS-REFERENCE
Putting in a lawn pages 38–40

Outlining and Improving Lawns

Information in Brief

Tools

Dethatcher (rent)
Aerator (hand tool)
Aerating or piercing boards
(homemade)
Rake, spade, spading fork
String
Edging tool or spade

Materials

Lawn edging tiles or stones
Edging band (metal, plastic)
Garden soil, sand

Time Expenditure

Placing edging stones:
1–2 hours per yard (meter)
Cutting edges:
20 minutes per yard (meter)
Dethatching (with raking):
30 minutes per 11 square
feet (m²)
Repairing damage:
About 1 hour per 11 square
feet (m²) (depending on
the damage)

Defined Lawn Boundaries

Edges set a boundary to the lawn and frame the picture. They also hinder the root competition from trees or of the lawn into scalloped beds. Natural and unobtrusive artificial stone (expensive) fits into most gardens easily; on the other hand, plain cement slabs look very severe. Inset, ribbon-like borders of metal or plastic are set in at soil level so you can go over them with the lawn mower or edge cutter.

Unedged Lawn Borders

If you reject the installation of a firm edging for aesthetic reasons, you should cut clean edges each spring. This is best done with a special edge cutter, but if necessary, it can also be done with a spade.

Stretch a string along the edge and cut the grass back at an angle (from the grass toward the bed). Curving lawn edges are cut "by feel" or marked with a string compass.

Lawn care also includes "surface cosmetics"—the repairing of mossy or damaged places and edging.

Repairing Damaged Spots

Damaged spots should be cut out shallowly (throw the sod onto the compost). Remove any remaining grass roots and dig the cleared area down for an inch or so (several centimeters).

Improving the Soil

Fill the cleared area with a mixture of garden soil and sand or cut away enough earth to make the upper edge of the trench (plus sod!) even with the lawn.

Restoring the Lawn Surface

With improvements after removal of superfluous soil or with depressions that have been filled in, refit the sod that was lifted and water thoroughly.

After the soil is improved, large areas of cut-away damage are either reseeded or healthy turf from a place along the edge is inserted.

Dethatching

Mossy places in the lawn are usually a sign of poor drainage and water collecting. Go over the surface with a dethatcher (thoroughly raking out the remnants), and sprinkle sand over the treated area. Work the sand lightly down into the soil with the rake. In small areas the ground can be carefully loosened with a spading fork, so-called aeration, or with home-made piercing boards and sand applied. On larger areas, the only remedy is to replace the soil and reseed.

Expert Tip
Moss killers are only a temporary solution.

Cross-References
String compass pages 28–29
Seeding lawns pages 38–39

Dividing and Staking Perennials

Information in Brief

Tools for Dividing

Spade
2 spading forks
Garden knife

Materials for Staking

Bamboo stakes
Metal hoop supports
Twig or stick system
Garden string

When to Divide?

Every 3–4 years (late summer
to early fall or spring)

When to Support?

Spring, when the plants are
putting out new growth

Time Expenditure

Division:
10 minutes per plant
Staking:
2–3 minutes for individual
supports, 10 minutes for
systems

Dividing Perennials

Work the spading fork in all around
the plant and lift the root system
from the ground. Pull apart loose root
systems with your hands or a garden
knife. Large, woody rootstocks are
divided with a hard blow of the spade
or with two spading forks inserted
back to back, which are then levered
apart. Then, using a garden knife,
cut off outside roots with a shoot
bud—these are replanted.

Staking Slender, Tall Perennials

Bamboo stakes are inexpensive, very
natural-looking supports that have
many uses. With tall plants (e.g.,
Fritellaria), poke a stake into the soil
and tie the plant to it with garden
string (in a figure-eight loop).

Division rejuvenates your plants, while staking keeps the fragile plants from breaking.

 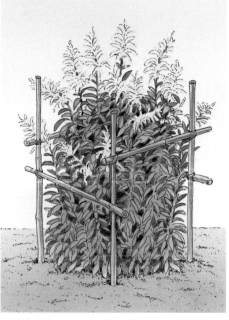 

Staking with Metal Hoops

One heavy summer thunderstorm can quickly mow down tall plants in a perennial bed. Prone plants that don't fully break in a storm may grow vertically, but develop a "kink," which cannot be corrected later. Stakes with metal rings are especially suitable for individual tall plants like delphinium.

Staking Wide Perennials

Plant supports should be effective but not noticeable. Large-spreading, dense clumps of rather tall perennials are best supported with a natural-looking framework of bamboo stakes. Put four stakes in the ground in a square (about 20 × 20 in [50 × 50 cm]) and fix horizontal stakes to them at an appropriate height (use baling wire). As needed put several "boxes" next to one another. The plants grow through the stakes and conceal them completely. You can also use Y-shaped branches set in soil around plants for natural-looking support.

Large-Area Supports

Commercially available staking systems are suitable when large-area supports are required. The system consists of vertical stakes that are linked together with hooked horizontal stakes. Perennials that grow in clumps are supported with a single stake to which rings of various diameters are attached (especially practical are rings with adjustable heights).

EXPERT TIP
Divide rhizomes into finger-length pieces.

CROSS-REFERENCE
Planting perennials pages 42–43

Staking and Protecting Trees and Shrubs

Information in Brief

Materials for Staking

Stake or stakes
8–12 in (20–30 cm) garden
hose or cuff
Burlap
Tree banding or jute string

Tools for Staking

Sledge hammer
Knife

Materials for Winter Protection

Bark mulch
Straw
Sturdy bamboo stakes
Baling wire
Burlap

Time Expenditure

Staking:
    Depending on construction,
    30 minutes to 1 hour
Winter protection:
    Mulching a bed, about
    20 minutes per 11 square
    feet (square meter); "tent"
    building 1 hour

Supporting Conifers
After planting, drive a stake into the ground at an angle (about 45°). The upper end of the supporting stake must point in the direction of the prevailing wind. The post should be brought close to the tree trunk and be seated firmly in the ground. Bind the stake firmly to the trunk of the tree with a band (tied in a figure eight). After a few weeks, when the soil has settled, check the positioning and correct the position of the tie.

Several Supports for Large Trees
With large trees or those that are particularly vulnerable to the wind, one stake is not enough. Drive three or four stakes into the ground close to the trunk and nail boards across the top to maintain the distance between them. Put a supporting brace (e.g., with a wire drawn through a piece of garden hose or plastic sleeve) around the tree trunk and attach it to the posts with wire or jute string.

**Tree supports keep the delicate
new roots from being torn by the
wind-blown movement of the trunk.**

Supporting Stakes for Small Trees

Small trees can be supported with a
post. Put a tree band or a jute string
around the trunk and fasten it to the
post. Protect the trunk the first winter with burlap wrapping or a plastic
sleeve especially if deer or rabbits
are a problem.

Cuff as Trunk Support

Use a rubber hose (nursery supply),
old bicycle tire, or a garden hose as
a cuff. With single supports, make a
figure eight of the supporting string
(rubber tubing).

Winter Protection

Tender shrubs must be protected
from frost during their early years.
Pack straw and spruce branches
between the branches and cover the
shrub with spruce branches.

   You achieve even better protection with a "teepee" of firm bamboo
stakes (tied together at the top).
Over this goes a "tarpaulin" of
burlap (old sacks) that is fastened
to the supports with wire.

Winter Protection

Heap the perennial you are protecting with soil and spread bark mulch
and leaves several inches (several
centimeters) deep on the bed (insu-
lation). Tie the branches together,
and wrap the entire thing with straw
matting or burlap.

EXPERT TIP
*Post length = trunk length +
root ball + 12 in (30 cm)*

CROSS-REFERENCES
Planting trees pages 52–53
Choosing plants pages 122–133

Pruning Trees

Information in Brief

Tools

Limbing saw
Clippers
Garden knife

Materials

Wound paint (optional)

Time to Do It

Fall or early spring

Time Expenditure

About 1 hour

Sawing Off a Branch: Step 1
Remove thick branches in three steps:

First, using a sharp limbing saw, make a cut from underneath to the middle of the branch (8 in [20 cm] from the trunk).

Sawing Off a Branch: Step 2
Now move the saw $^1/_2$–$^3/_4$ in (1–2 cm) further toward the outside, and saw the limb here from the top down.

If the branch doesn't break on its own, carefully help it along.

Left: Ragged cut edges heal poorly.
Center: The cut is too far above the side bud.
Right: Correct cut.

The alpha and omega of successful tree pruning are sharp pruners and the correctly made cut.

Sawing Off a Branch: Step 3
After the large portion of the branch is cut off, you can go into detail:

To finish, make a third cut, as neatly as possible, close to the stem.

Make sure when cutting branches that you have a firm foothold, especially if the branch is high up on the tree. Check your tools for sharpness ahead of time.

Smoothing the Wound Edges
Using a sharp garden knife, carve the edges smooth. Remove all splinters and bumps down to the bark. The wound surface should be as smooth and clean as possible, so that there are as few chances for water or fungus infection to enter as possible.

Sealing the Wound
While some professional arborists no longer advise sealing wounds, some still recommend this practice. To do so, after cutting, seal the wound surface with tree wound paint; particularly easy to use are tubes from which the paint can be squirted directly onto the wound.

Clean Wound Healing
A clean, smooth, and thoroughly sealed wound closing is the best life insurance for your tree.

EXPERT TIP
Ask about pruning when buying trees and shrubs.

CROSS-REFERENCES
Planting trees pages 52–53
Choosing plants pages 124–125

Clipping Hedges

Information in Brief

Tools

Manual hedge clippers
Electric hedge clippers
Pruning shears
Stepladder or scaffold
String and stakes
Spirit level
Gloves
Safety glasses

When to Prune

Deciduous hedges:
Fall or spring; large hedges
(after birds have hatched);
again in July or August

Evergreen hedges:
Late fall or early spring

Time Expenditure

About 20 minutes per yard
(meter) of hedge

Pruning Young Hedges
Immediately after planting, the main shoots of a deciduous or evergreen hedge are cut back by half. They are pruned again the next fall so that the hedge will grow thick later. Shorten all side shoots and cut the tallest growing shoots at the top to a uniform height.

Don't use hedge clippers for this job but use sharp pruning shears and take it branch by branch.

Hedge Pruning the First Few Years
Since a hedge often grows a little irregularly in the first few years, you can correct it in a timely fashion with hand pruners and loppers. Prune the top of the hedge smooth and pay attention to long, extending shoots, which can be shortened with the pruners.

A rule of thumb is that the side shoots of neighboring shrubs should grow in among each other.

In the first two years, hedges are trimmed with loppers or hand clippers, and only afterward with a power clipper.

Regular Hedge Trimming

When your hedge is established, it is pruned regularly. Electric clippers need a sufficiently long cord (belt sling, belt mount). Battery-operated tools free you of the cord; check when buying, however, to find out how long a battery charge lasts. For very long hedges, of course, you can also fall back on a gas-powered clipper. Stretch a string at the planned final height of the hedge (use a spirit level).

Hedge Pruning

On the top surface, cut the hedge straight along the string. Then cut the side walls of the hedge smooth from top to bottom.

Be careful about safety! Wear gloves, sturdy but comfortable clothing, and also wear safety glasses. With high hedges always use a stable scaffold. Deciduous hedge cuttings go on the compost heap or, slightly rotted, can be used as mulch on shrubbery beds or under the hedge.

Box Cut

Every hedge gets more sun, water, and nutrients at its upper parts. If it is kept too narrow in its lower regions, it will easily become bare. Cut deciduous hedges in trapezoidal or box form.

Trapezoidal Cut

Evergreen hedges are basically cut in a trapezoidal form, which may, however, then be cut off when a hedge has reached its final height.

Expert Tip
Be very careful about safety.

Cross-References
Planting hedges pages 50–51
Choosing plants pages 126–131

Pruning and Protecting Roses

Information in Brief

Tools

Sharp pruning shears
Gloves

Materials

Mulch
Straw
Spruce branches
Burlap sacking

Time for Pruning

Spring:
Wild or species roses, once- and ever-blooming shrub roses, climbing roses, bedding roses, and hybrid teas
Summer:
Ever-blooming shrub and climbing roses

Time Expenditure

About 20 minutes per bush

Ground Rules for Pruning Roses

It should be the goal of pruning to achieve a loose growth form of main canes, from which the flower-bearing branches will grow. Use sharp pruning shears, which leave the cut surface smooth, and cut at a slant over an eye. First remove old, bare, and dead main canes. Then all remaining main canes are cut back to a height of 12–20 in (30–50 cm) (with large shrub roses it is all right for the canes to be left longer). Now, do you still see any branches that are growing across another one? Remove these too. The remaining canes should stand away from one another in a fan shape and not get in each other's way.

Once-blooming roses (ask when purchasing) bloom on the short branches from old wood. Such roses are only thinned out every few years, since otherwise they would flower too little.

Rose pruning is not a secret science for specialists. The best way to develop the necessary experience is by doing it.

Deadheading
With ever-blooming roses, continually remove the spent flowers in order to stimulate formation of new ones. Cut the stems of single flowers or bunched flowers just over the next lower completely developed leaf.

Cutting Out Wild Shoots
Sometimes the wild or species rose rootstock onto which the hybrid tea is grafted will put out wild shoots from below the bud union. Scratch away the soil down to the bud union and cut off the wild shoots.

Supporting Standard Roses
Tall tree roses always need a firm support. Plan to install a post at planting to which the thin stem can be securely fastened with a broad rubber band or a cuff.

You can also make a support of several thin posts.

Winter Protection
Roses are susceptible to frost damage, so winter protection is required. Heap up mulch (6–8 in [15–20 cm]) high over the lower region of the shrub. Lay straw and some spruce branches over it. In addition, it is recommended that you make a covering for the canes of climbing roses with spruce branches or burlap sacking (tied with garden string).

The bud union of tree roses is located on the trunk, so this area must be especially protected with straw, spruce branches, or burlap sacking.

EXPERT TIP
Use complete fertilizer in spring, potassium-magnesium fertilizer in late summer.

CROSS-REFERENCES
Planting roses pages 48–49
Choosing plants pages 134–139

The Garden Year— Calendar of Jobs

Month	Flowers and Shrubs	Garden Job
January–February 	Press heaved plants back into soil; shrubs transplanted; sow seeds of first annuals indoors; free shrubs of snow accumulation. Check mulch; add extra if needed.	Now is the best time to study garden books and catalogs. Now at the latest, protect perennial and shrub borders against late frosts. Sharpen and repair garden tools.
March 	Plant perennials on mild days; cut back ornamental grasses to the ground; prune roses. Fertilize perennial and shrub borders with organic fertilizer.	In mild areas, remove winter protection. Begin weeding now. Remove fallen twigs, leaves, and branches from garden.
April 	Sow annuals out-of-doors; plant perennials; unhill the roses.	In severe areas, remove winter protection. Tidy up the lawn and fertilize. Mulch beds; turn compost.
May–June 	Plant dahlias and gladiolas; plant rhododendron and azaleas (twist out wilted flowers). Remove flowers, later the withered leaves of spring bulbs. Plant the annuals started indoors.	Mow lawn. Water trees and shrubs in dry spells. Put in supports for perennials. Fertilize perennial beds once more. Look for pests and deal with them. Loosen soil and do weeding.

Certain jobs should be completed at certain times, if possible. The Job Calendar tells you when.

Month	Flowers and Shrubs	Garden Job
July–August 	Regularly deadhead ever-blooming roses, perennials, annuals. Sow biennials outdoors. Plant conifers. Fertilize roses with potassium-magnesium fertilizer (July).	Prune deciduous arborvitae (*Thuja*), and spruce hedges. Watch for pests and deal with them.
September 	Plant bulbs, tubers, and corms of spring flowers. Plant perennials. Plant conifers and broad-leaved evergreens.	Fix lawn or seed a new one. Remove weeds from beds.
October 	Plant roses, deciduous woody shrubs, and last bulbs, tubers, and corms. Cut back perennial borders and cover with mulch for the winter. Dig out dahlias and gladiolas.	Turn compost. Rake leaves. Now is a good time for construction projects in the yard and garden.
November–December 	Hill the roses and protect for the winter. Tie up tall grasses (frost protection).	Finally prepare beds for the winter. Leave grasses and perennials with interesting flower heads till spring (they act as bird feeders and are attractive covered with frost). Order seed catalogs for next year.

Choosing Plants

Choosing Plants

Look for the Appropriate Species

Humankind has been striving since ancient times to select and breed plants with particularly good qualities for the garden. Explorers brought new plant species back from their travels. Today, botanists continue to discover new plants, and through hybridization, have developed unimaginable varieties of garden plants. Equally as important as the impressive variety of garden plants is the fact that this variety is available to everyone.

The Structure of the Portrait Section

The following pages can offer hardly more than a broad overview. The selection presented here consists mostly of easy-care species and varieties that are available from all nurseries and mail order companies. Obviously you can look in the catalogs for other plants appropriate to your growing area that will be good in your garden. Thus your garden will become a unique showplace. The portrait section is organized according to the following scheme:

▶ First the spring, summer, and fall flowers are introduced in large groups. This makes it easier to choose plants so you can have something in bloom in your flower beds during the entire growing season. These are followed by grasses, ferns, and ground covers, which can be combined well with flowering plants and exert their charm mainly through their growth habits. Trees and shrubs as well as roses are discussed separately because they create the basic structure of the garden with their woody, permanent growth. Finally come the high-growing climbing plants, which you can use to establish vertical accents.

The Winter Garden

In planning a garden it is easy to forget that during the cold season dormancy dominates in nature. Here are some suggestions so that your garden will also be a feast for the eyes in winter: In choosing woody plants, look for interesting growth forms. Artistically branching limbs, for instance, have their own special charm, especially when covered with frost or snow.

Bark colors offer visual interest in the wintery grayness, like the white anthracite of birches, the red or green of *Cornus* species, as well as berries that persist. Also select evergreen woody plants and perennials. After the leaves fall, they dominate the garden scene. Don't clean up too thoroughly in the fall! Let the grasses and perennials with attractive growth forms stay until spring. Winter-proof garden elements like statues, pergolas, and trellises are much more noticeable now.

▶ The plant portraits are broken down as follows: After the common name comes the internationally understood Latin name. Garden centers, catalogs, and books will sometimes use this name. It is best to use the Latin names of plants so you are assured of getting the right plant or correct information. Names of cultivars are in single quotation marks.

The details of height and width permit knowledgeable planning of distinctive staggering of heights in the border, and the width also affects the distance between plants. The numbers should be understood as averages, which may vary depending on variety, location, and soil. The same goes for the notations about blooming season that follow this information.

The next line gives information about the life form of the plant, for example, whether it is an annual or perennial. You will find the general planting and care instructions in the plant care section.

The pictograms (see right) indicate at a glance the most important requirements and characteristics of the plant. Then comes a note about any particularly noteworthy characteristic.

The Pictograms Used

 The plant thrives best in full sun

 The plant thrives best in part shade

 The plant thrives well even in shade

 Water the plant a lot (in general, daily)

 Water the plant moderately (about every 3–4 days)

 Water the plant very little (only during long dry spells)

 The plant has a spectacular effect when used alone

 The plant attracts attention with strikingly beautiful foliage

 The plant has particularly attractive fruits

 The plant contains poisonous or irritating substances

In the text that follows you find the following notations:

Flowers: Here the colors are noted, as well as the average diameter in paren-

On the following pages, you will find well-thought-out plant selections, from low ground covers to high-climbing vines.

theses (Ø). This allows you to create successful combinations with other plants in shades that go with it.
Soil: The customary location characteristics are listed. With their help you can judge whether the plant will do well for you without a lot of maintenance.
Care: Under this heading are special notes that do not appear in the plant care section.
Design: Here you find important tips

about how to use the plant to best effect.
Zone: Indicates the climate zone(s) in which a plant will thrive. Select only plants that will be comfortable in the prevailing climate. Check the Zone Map on p. 189 to see which zone number(s) correspond to your geographic location.

Below the colored rule there is occasionally a note about a good partner or additional expert tips.

SEE PAGES 56–74
Everything about the care of garden plants

Spring Flowers

Spring flowers, the first spots of color, put an end to the dominance of dreary tones in the garden. Therefore great importance is attached to this plant group.

Spring flowers like tulips and daffodils are primarily a matter of bulbs, corms, or tubers, which use the nutrients stored in that organ for their early growth. They are planted during their dormant period in the fall. Most species have retained their natural appearance and show off best in groups.

Along the Edges of Shrubbery and in the Lawn

An ideal place for them is under and around deciduous shrubs. If you leave the fallen leaves there, they form a natural mulch layer in which these plants do particularly well.

When the shrubs put out their leaves, the flowering period of these species has usually come to an end. They should now be able to go dormant, gathering all the important nutrients from the withering leaves and storing them in the bulb, corm, or tuber. If you leave the plants to themselves, many will spread by means of daughter bulbs or seeds and so develop natural-looking groups. Only hybrid forms of crocus, tulips, and narcissus must be replaced every few years.

Spring flowers can also be used to good effect in the lawn or along the edges of it. But wait to mow these strips until the leaves have faded and shriveled.

In Beds and Borders

Spring flowers also fit well into beds and borders. An ideal situation is to plant them where they can be seen through a window, for it's usually too cold to enjoy them from the patio or terrace. However, make sure that after the bulbs, corms, or tubers have finished and disappeared, there aren't empty spaces in the planting area. You should plant the area with companion perennials whose foliage will cover the empty spaces. Annual summer flowers also offer an alternative.

Bulbs, corms, and tubers provide the first flower fireworks in the garden year.

The First Messengers of Spring

Christmas Rose
Helleborus species and hybrids
Height/Width: 6–24 in (16–60 cm)/
12–32 in (30–80 cm)
Blooms: December–April
Perennial

▶ **attractive, large flowers**

Flowers: White, yellow, yellowish-green, pink, red, or purple (Ø 1$\frac{1}{2}$–2$\frac{3}{4}$ in [4–7 cm]). **Soil:** Humusy, fresh, loamy, containing lime. **Care:** Plant in fall, cut off dead leaves in spring; water during spring dry spells; leave undisturbed and try not to disturb the roots with digging. **Design:** With enough space, combine several species, hybrids, and varieties with differing flower colors; especially beautiful underneath flowering shrubs or between spring bulbs. **Zone:** 4–8.

Species Crocus
Crocus tommasinianus
Height/Width: 2–4 in (5–10 cm)/
2–3 in [5–7.5 cm])
Blooms: February–April
Corm

▶ **spreads fast**

Flowers: White, light violet, or blue with glowing yellow stamens (Ø 1–1$\frac{1}{4}$ in [3–4 cm]). **Soil:** Any normal, good, well-drained soil, which may even be sandy or stony, with the exception of a very dry location.
Care: Plant the hazelnut-sized bulbs in late summer or fall and fertilize until flowering; water during spring dry spells. **Design:** Especially decorative in groups under shrubs or with other spring flowers along the edges of the lawn. **Zone:** 3–8.

Snowdrops
Galanthus nivalis
Height/Width: 4–6 in (10–15 cm)/
4 in (10 cm)
Blooms: February–April
Bulb

▶ **trouble-free plant**

Flowers: Nodding, white, but the three inner petals have a charming green spot, delicately fragrant (Ø $\frac{1}{4}$ in [1 cm]). **Soil:** Fresh or at least spring moist, rich in humus, loamy; it will not tolerate any dry, sandy soils. **Care:** Plant bulbs in fall, for propagating bulb clumps dig out after flowering, divide, and replant. **Design:** Always plant in loose groups, which over the course of time will form larger groups by themselves. **Zone:** 3–9.

EXPERT TIP
Pictured is the beautiful hybrid 'Atrorubens'.

GOOD PARTNERS
Winter aconite, Christmas rose

Early bloomers stockpile nutrients in their storage organs for the necessary start before other plants. Under open shrubbery they display the full glory of their flowers.

Squill

Scilla siberica, shown: 'Spring Beauty'
Height/Width: 4–6 in (10–15 cm)/
2–3 in (5–8 cm)
Blooms: March–April
Bulb

▶ **very attractive in groups**

Flowers: White, pink, pale purple to blue (Ø $^1/_4$–$^1/_2$ in [1–1.5 cm]). **Soil:** Well-drained, humusy garden soil, which should be neither too soggy nor too dry. **Care:** Plant the bulbs in the fall, mulch with compost in February or apply organic fertilizer; water during spring dry spells. **Design:** Ideal for naturalizing on the edges of wooded areas or in combination with narcissi, crocus, primulas, and tulips as colorful groups in the border; also suitable for the rock garden. **Zone:** 4–8.

Spring Snowflake

Leucojum vernum
Height/Width: 8 in (20 cm)/4–6 in (10 15 cm)
Blooms: February–April
Bulb

▶ **one of the earliest to flower**

Flowers: White, but the tips of the petals have yellow to yellow-green spots, fragrant, nodding (Ø $^1/_2$ in [1.5 cm]). **Soil:** Damp—above all in a sunny location, containing humus, loamy if possible—but no sandy soils; also tolerates occasional flooding. **Care:** Plant bulbs in late summer to fall, add some organic-chemical fertilizer until flowering, let naturalize undisturbed. **Design:** Plant in large groups under woody plants, also very attractive along ponds, in the bog garden, or close to the house. **Zone:** 4–8.

Winter Aconite

Eranthis hyemalis
Height/Width: 2–4 in (5–10 cm)/
2$^1/_2$ in (6 cm)
Blooms: February–March
Bulb

▶ **spreads by means of seeds**

Flowers: Brilliant yellow with yellow stamens and a wreath of fringed bright green bracts, pleasantly fragrant (Ø $^1/_2$–1 in [2–2.5 cm]). **Soil:** Fresh, humusy and well-drained, never dry, compacted, or soggy. **Care:** Plant the bulbs in the fall during their dormancy; they must not be already dried out; water during spring dry spells. **Design:** Best to locate in large groups under lacy shrubbery; they naturalize easily if they are allowed to grow undisturbed. **Zone:** 5–9.

EXPERT TIP
The summer snowflake (L. aestivum) blooms April–June.

GOOD PARTNERS
Spring-flowering crocus, snowdrops

Spring Flower Carpets

Aubrieta

Aubrieta deltoidea, shown 'Moerheimii'
Height/Width: 2–6 in (5–15 cm)/ 20–24 in (50–60 cm)
Blooms: April–May
Cushion perennial

▶ **glorious curtain of flowers**

Flowers: According to variety, pink, velvet red, lavender blue, violet (Ø about 1/4 in [1 cm]). **Soil:** Well-drained, moderately dry; rich, chalky, heavy soils unsuitable. **Care:** Some fertilizer in spring (not later), water only during long dry spells, cut back after flowering; the pink- and red-flowered varieties are certainly very attractive but are much shorter-lived than the blue and violet ones.
Design: Grows flowing over landings, on tops of walls, in rock gardens, also as a low border plant for beds.
Zone: 4–9.

Perennial Candytuft

Iberis sempervirens
Height/Width: 6–12 in (15–30 cm)/ 12–24 in (30–60 cm)
Blooms: April–May
Perennial-like subshrub

▶ **trouble-free, long-lived plant**

Flowers: White, also pink, in dense cymes (Ø up to 1/4 in [1 cm]).
Soil: Well-drained, somewhat dry, sandy, poor in humus and nutrients.
Care: Fertilize in spring with some compost, otherwise use no fertilizer; cut back old plants to about half every few years to prevent balding; in very cold winters cover the evergreen plants with branches.
Design: Ideal for slopes and path edging, for the rock garden, and as bed definers. **Zone:** 3–9.

Grape Hyacinths

Muscari armeniacum
Height/Width: 6–8 in (15–20 cm)/ 3–4 in (8–10 cm)
Blooms: April–May
Bulb

▶ **naturalizes easily**

Flowers: Intense cobalt blue with white edge, also light and sky-blue varieties; strongly fragrant (small round flowers in 2-in- [5-cm-] high inflorescences). **Soil:** Well-drained, tolerates dryness. **Care:** Plant bulbs in late summer; they are sensitive to drying out; let the leaves die back after flowering; if the plants are not disturbed they will spread through bulb offsets. **Design:** Very valuable for rock gardens; also ideal under shrubs and along the edges of fields.
Zone: 5–8.

GOOD PARTNERS
Rock cress, perennial candytuft, bearded iris

GOOD PARTNERS
Forsythia, early tulips, and narcissi

These species bring color into the garden. Plant them in large groups between later-flowering perennials. They become striking islands of color.

Trumpet Daffodils
Narcissus hybrids, shown: 'Golden Harvest'
Height/Width: 16 20 in (40 50 cm)/ 4–6 in (10–15 cm)
Blooms: March–April
Bulb

▶ **many good, inexpensive varieties**

Flowers: Yellow, also white and bicolored varieties (Ø 2–2³/4 in [5–7 cm]). **Soil:** Well-drained and never soggy, damp to somewhat dry, sandy to humusy, neutral to slightly acid, rich in nutrients. **Care:** Plant bulbs in fall, water the foliage and flowers in spring during dry spells; best fertilized with compost when new growth appears; do not use chemical fertilizers. **Design:** Beautiful with other spring flowers in beds and borders, also along the edges of woods. **Zone:** 3–9.

Windflowers
Anemone blanda
Height/Width: 4–6 in (10–15 cm)/ 3–4 in (8–10 cm)
Blooms: March–May
Corm

▶ **forms attractive groups**

Flowers: Blue, also white and pink varieties and some of those with a white eye (Ø 1 in [2–3 cm]). **Soil:** Well-drained, not too damp, humusy, slightly chalky. **Care:** Plant corms in fall, let soak in water for a day beforehand; if possible do not disturb or dig in the vicinity. **Design:** Thrives under shrubs, in the foreground and along the edges of beds—however, do not plant near fruit trees, since plum rust can over-winter on anemone roots. **Zone:** 5–8.

Crown-Imperial
Fritillaria imperialis
Height/Width: 24–39 in (60–100 cm)/ 8–10 in (20–25 cm)
Blooms: April
Bulb

▶ **creates a strong accent**

Flowers: Depending on variety, yellow, orange-red, or red (Ø 1¹/2–2 in [4–5 cm]). **Soil:** Deeply dug, well-drained, and light, rich. **Care:** Plant the fist-sized bulbs from August to September, fertilize in spring, water well during dry spells in the growing season; cut back faded flowers to the first leaves on the stalk; only remove leaves after they have yellowed; cover in fall with mature compost. **Design:** Beautiful in small groups as focal points in perennial beds. **Zone:** 5–9.

EXPERT TIP
There are countless other varieties of narcissus.

GOOD PARTNERS
European wood anemone (A. nemorosa), small narcissi

Multiplicity of Tulips

Single-flowered Tulips

Variety Group	Flower Color Flower Form	Height/in (cm) When Flowering
'Apricot Beauty' Single early	apricot cup-shaped	10–16 (25–40) April
'Pax' Triumph	pure white cup-shaped	16–24 (40–60) April–May
'Cassini' Triumph	blood red cup-shaped	16–24 (40–60) April–May
'Apeldoorn' Darwin hybrid	orange-black saucer-shaped	16–24 (40–60) April–May
'Elizabeth Arden' Darwin hybrid	salmon pink saucer-shaped	16–24 (40–60) April–May
'Sorbet' Single late	white and red cup-shaped	20–28 (50–70) May
'Maytime' Lily-flowered	mauve with white lily-like	20–26 (50–65) May
'West Point' Lily-flowered	bright yellow lily-like	20–26 (50–65) May
'Blue Parrot' Parrot	violet-blue wavy and fringed	12–24 (30–60) May
'White Parrot' Parrot	white wavy and fringed	12–24 (30–60) May
'Arma' Crispa	scarlet fringed	12–24 (30–70) May
'Hamilton' Crispa	golden yellow fringed	12–24 (30–70) May

Double-flowered Tulips

'Electra' Double early	cherry-red saucer-shaped	10–14 (25–35) April
'Orange Nassau' Double early	deep red saucer-shaped	10–14 (25–35) April
'Peach Blossom' Double early	rose red saucer-shaped	10–14 (25–35) April
'Schoonoord' Double early	white saucer-shaped	10–14 (25–35) April
'Angelique' Double late	pale pink peony-flowered	16–24 (40–60) May
'Gold Medal' Double late	golden yellow peony-flowered	16–24 (40–60) May
'Mount Tacoma' Double late	white peony-flowered	16–24 (40–60) May

Botanical Tulips

Tulipa kaufmannniana hybrids
Height/Width: 6–12 in (15–30 cm)/ 4–6 in (10–15 cm)
Blooms: March–April
Bulbs

▶ **flower particularly early**

Flowers: The many varieties of hybrids are usually bicolored in white, yellow, orange, pink, apricot, red, and scarlet; the flowers open to a star shape in the sunshine (Ø 2–3 in [5–8 cm]). **Soil:** Well-drained, rich; ideally neutral to slightly acid garden soil. **Care:** Plant bulbs in fall; fertilize when new growth appears; provide damp soil at flowering time, then let stay dry; cut back stems when flowering is finished. **Design:** Ideal for the rock garden or beds, pots, and flower boxes. **Zone:** 4–9.

Single Early Tulips

Tulipa, shown: 'Coleur Cardinal'
Height/Width: 10–16 in (25–40 cm)/ 4–6 in (10–15 cm)
Blooms: April
Bulb

▶ **provide early color**

Flowers: All colors except blue, from white, yellow, orange, pink, to red and purple (Ø to 2^1/$_2$ in [6 cm]). **Soil:** Moderately dry to fresh, but not soggy, sandy-loamy, rich in nutrients but poor in humus, neutral to slightly acid. **Care:** Plant bulbs in fall, fertilize during growing period, provide sufficient moisture during flowering, remove spent flowers, let foliage go dormant. **Design:** For colorful spring beds and borders, also in planters or pots and grown for cut flowers. **Zone:** 4–5–8.

GOOD PARTNERS
Cushion perennials, crocus, grape hyacinths

Tulips show off best in loose groups, so you should always plant several bulbs of the same variety and coordinate the heights and colors.

Double Late Tulips

Tulipa, shown: 'Orange Princess'
Height/Width: 15–24 in (40–60 cm)/
4–6 in (10 15 cm)
Blooms: May
Bulb

▶ **splendid, protect from wind**

Flowers: Depending on variety, cream white, golden yellow, red and crimson, also with borders or centers of other colors (Ø to 3 in [8 cm]). **Soil:** Moderately dry to fresh, but not soggy, sandy-loamy, rich in nutrients but humus-poor, not too alkaline. **Care:** Plant bulbs in fall, fertilize during growing season, support in windy locations, remove spent flowers, let go dormant. **Design:** Especially beautiful in loose groups in the perennial bed together with color-coordinated flowers of late spring. **Zone:** 3/4–8.

Viridiflora Tulips

Tulipa, shown: 'Hummingbird'
Height/Width: 12–20 in (30–50 cm)/
4–6 in (10–15 cm)
Blooms: May
Bulb

▶ **delicately colored, many new varieties**

Flowers: Broken shades, yellow, salmon-pink, purple, always with bright-to-dark-green stripes or flamed markings (Ø 3–4 in [8–10 cm]). **Soil:** Normal garden soil, not too damp or at all soggy. **Care:** Plant bulbs in fall, fertilize during growing season and water during dry spells, cut off spent flowers, and let leaves die back. **Design:** Put them in pastel-colored, color-matched groups in spring beds and borders. **Zone:** 3/4–8.

Parrot Tulips

Tulipa, shown: 'Flaming Parrot'
Height/Width: 16–24 in (40–60 cm)/
4–6 in (10 15 cm)
Blooms: May
Bulb

▶ **striking flowers**

Flowers: Multicolored in very strong colors like white, yellow, orange, red, purple, and brown-red, often flamed; the edges of the petals are fringed (Ø about 3–4 in [8–10 cm]). **Soil:** Any normal garden soil that isn't too damp, nutrient-rich but poor in humus. **Care:** Plant bulbs in fall, fertilize in spring until new growth appears, support in windy locations or plant between protecting perennials; cut off spent flowers. **Design:** Because of the striking flowers, use in the foreground of the beds. **Zone:** 4–7.

EXPERT TIP
Other varieties: 'Bonanza' (red/yellow), 'Golden Nice' (yellow)

EXPERT TIP
Other varieties: 'Fantasy' (pink, 24 in [60 cm])/'Rococo' (crimson, 14 in [35 cm])

Spring Finale

Tall Bearded Iris

Iris hybrids
Height/Width: 24–48 in (60–120 cm)/
6 in (15 cm)
Blooms: May–June
Perennial

▶ **numerous varieties available**

Flowers: Except for pure red, all
colors from white to purple and
brown, petals often different colors
(Ø 3–4 in [8–10 cm]). **Soil:** Dry,
well-drained, rich in nutrients but
lean in humus, sandy, somewhat
alkaline. **Care:** In fall, plant the
rhizome shallowly so that about
half the rhizome shows above ground;
remove dead leaves in spring; fertilize
with compost. **Design:** Especially
beautiful in groups of several colors
(contrasting or tone on tone) in
the background of a sunny bed.
Zone: 3–9.

Aquilegia

Aquilegia vulgaris and *Aquilegia* hybrids
Height/Width: 16–32 in (40–80 cm)/
12–18 in (30–45 cm)
Blooms: May–June
Perennial

▶ **very beautiful wild perennial**

Flowers: Blue-purple, hybrids in
white, yellow, pink, red, light blue,
and very often also bicolored (Ø
about 2 in [5 cm]). **Soil:** Rich in
humus, loose, and fresh. **Care:** Water
in dry spells, thin the self-sown
seedlings, replant the extra plants
or put on the compost heap.
Design: The wild form looks especially
charming in natural gardens, also in
combination with woody plants and
along the edge of a wood; the hybrid
varieties also form focal points in
perennial borders. **Zone:** 4–9.

Common Garden Peonies

Paeonia lactiflora hybrids, shown 'Holbein'
Height/Width: 20–43 in (50–110 cm)/
24–35 in (60–90 cm)
Blooms: May–June
Perennial

▶ **long-lived plant**

Flowers: White, pink, red, also
bicolored, partially double, delicately
fragranced (Ø about 4 in [10 cm]).
Soil: Moderately dry to moist, rich
in nutrients, humus, loose, deeply
cultivated, slightly alkaline. **Care:**
Plant in early fall; in spring and
again in early fall, give compost,
rotted manure, or organic fertilizers
like horn shavings; support tall
plants; water in dry spells during
the blooming season; remove spent
flowers. **Design:** As commanding
focal point in perennial border or
cottage garden. **Zone:** 3–8.

GOOD PARTNERS
Flax, poppies, candytuft,
spurge [euphorbia]

GOOD PARTNERS
Anemones, ferns, hosta,
geranium [cranesbill]

When choosing late-flowering species, remember that they must also harmonize well with the first flowers of early summer.

Sweet William
Dianthus barbatus
Height/Width: 20–24 in (50–60 cm)/ 8–12 in (20–30 cm)
Blooms: May–August
Biennial

▶ **good cut flowers**

Flowers: White, pink, red to dark red, also bi- and multicolored markings, single or double, intensely fragrant (Ø about 1/4 in [1 cm]). **Soil:** Well-drained, nutrient-rich, normal garden soil; but loamy sandy preferred.
Care: Sow for flowers the next year in June–July; in exposed situations cover young plants in winter; in spring give some fertilizer; water moderately while growing. **Design:** Outstandingly suitable for the flower bed; place in groups between other annuals or perennials. **Zone:** 4–9.

Forget-me-nots
Myosotis sylvatica
Height/Width: 6–12 in (15–30 cm)/ 6 in (15 cm)
Blooms: May–August
Biennials

▶ **self-sows vigorously**

Flowers: Sky-blue, also white and pink varieties; eye yellowish or orange-yellow (Ø 5 mm). **Soil:** Nutrient-rich, loose, and humusy, prefers somewhat loamy, moist. **Care:** Sow in July for flowers the next year; in exposed situations, cover during the winter; fertilize in spring; water in dry spells.
Design: Very beautiful along paths or as trimming around the edge of a bed; also pretty in ribbons between tulips, narcissi, and later crocuses; also suitable for balcony flower boxes and as cut flowers. **Zone:** 4–8.

Oriental Poppies
Papaver orientale, shown 'Frührot'
Height/Width: 12–39 in (30–100 cm)/ 24 in (60 cm)
Blooms: May–June
Perennial

▶ **magnificent, short-lived flowers**

Flowers: Depending on the variety, white, pink, orange to red, and to some degree also petals veined or flecked with other colors (Ø up to 6 in [15 cm]). **Soil:** Well-drained, deeply cultivated, dry to fresh, but never soggy. **Care:** Fertilize with compost when new growth appears; cut off spent flowers, but if you want to collect seeds, let some seed capsules ripen; cover in winter in exposed situations. **Design:** Works best as a tall lead plant in the background of the border. **Zone:** 3–7.

GOOD PARTNERS
Hollyhocks, campanulas, other carnations

EXPERT TIP
Good varieties: 'Blue Ball' (blue), 'Carmine King' (pink)

Summer Flowers

This plant group offers an enchanting variety of flower and growth forms. Summer's warmth and long daylight hours help create their brilliant colors.

With the finale of spring, the great season of the garden begins: As the last spring flowers fade, the summer flowers put out their shoots, and here and there the first flowers are already showing. At this time, too, it is still possible to visit the garden center to look for suitable container plants, which can be transplanted almost all year long in milder climates, and into the fall in colder areas. The plant portraits on the following pages should help you to furnish a variety of beds with an attractive display of summer-flowering plants. Even a brief look around at the variety in a nursery, however, will show you that far more plant choices are available.

Tips for Buying

Even if it looks ever so enticing, don't let yourself be mindlessly "seduced" by a particular plant. Always keep in mind the theme of your garden: Will this plant fit in with the color scheme of the ones you already have? Will its height fit in with the wavy up-and-down of your bed? Will it provide an interesting growth form or pretty foliage for a pleasant livening up of your flower bed?

In any case, you should also consider having some annual and biennial plants. Almost always there are some heavily blooming species and varieties among them that provide floods of color. Unlike perennials, which remain in the same location year round, these short-lived representatives of the plant world are replaced or resown year after year. You can also try sowing them yourself—plant seed is inexpensive and plentiful. Then study your finished bed and note the successful and less successful plants for the following year.

A foaming display of summer flower glory, even in front of a fence.

The First Early Summer Flowers

Tussock Campanula
Campanula carpatica
Height/Width: 8–12 in (20–30 cm)/
16–20 in (40–50 cm)
Blooms: June–August
Cushion perennial

▶ **flowers for a long time, self-sows**

Flowers: Depending on the variety, violet to blue, also silver-blue and white (Ø to 1¹/₂ in [4 cm]). **Soil:** Well-drained, moderately dry to fresh, but the plants also tolerate dry, alkaline, and poor soils; they should not be in soggy soils. **Care:** Not too much fertilizer, otherwise it loses its compact cushiony form; water only during long dry spells; remove spent flowers. **Design:** As cushion in rock garden and in pockets in dry walls, in the foreground of perennial borders. **Zone:** 4–8.

Day Lily
Hemerocallis hybrids; shown 'Turned on'
Height/Width: 16–39 in (40–100 cm)/
16–24 in (40–60 cm)
Blooms: May–August
Perennial

▶ **large flowers, grassy leaves**

Flowers: Cream-white, yellow, orange, pink, red, violet, brown, almost black, also bicolors (Ø to 6 in [15 cm]). **Soil:** Moderately dry to moist; the species also tolerates damp locations; nutrient-rich, loamy; less abundantly flowering in shady locations. **Care:** Water during extended dry spells; fertilize now and again; remove spent flowers.
Design: Beautiful in groups at the water's edge or as lead plants in beds; the strap-like foliage produces interesting accents. **Zone:** 3–9.

Pot Marigold
Calendula officinalis
Height/Width: 12–28 in (30–70 cm)/
6–8 in (15–20 cm)
Blooms: June–September
Annual

▶ **ancient healing plant, trouble-free**

Flowers: Depending on variety, cream, yellow, orange to orange-red, sometimes with a brown center, single, semidouble, and double (Ø 2 in [5 cm]). **Soil:** Nutrient-rich but not too rich in nitrogen, loose, also somewhat dry, but no standing water. **Care:** Sow April–May; in following years the plants appear by themselves, self-sown; provide with compost in spring; remove spent flowers. **Design:** Ideal in cottage garden, beautiful also in dense groups or loosely scattered in the flower bed; very good cut flower.

EXPERT TIP
Relatives: Canterbury Bells, 24–48 in (60–120 cm), Peach-leaved Bellflower

GOOD PARTNERS
Delphinium, sage, rudbeckia, bog-star

A "colorful" area in itself is not yet a pretty flower bed. Tall, narrow plants divide it and create effective accents.

Foxglove
Digitalis purpurea
Height/Width: 39–55 in (100–140 cm)/ 12–16 (30–40 cm)
Blooms: June–July
Bi- to triennial

► **self-sows vigorously**

Flowers: Depending on variety, white, yellow, pink, and reddish purple, spotted (Ø 1–1¹/₂ in [3–4 cm], 12–16-in [30–40-cm] -high inflorescence).
Soil: Moderately dry to fresh, rich in humus, loamy, low in lime. **Care:** Sow from April; provide with compost in spring; remove spent flowers; when cut back after flowering it blooms again the following year. **Design:** Very effective along the edges of woods and in the natural garden; also ideal in the cottage garden; makes an accent in the background of the border; good cut flower. **Zone:** 4.

Wax Begonia
Begonia x semperflorens
Height/Width: 6–12 in (15–30 cm)/ 6–14 in (15–35 cm)
Blooms: June–November
Annual

► **versatile annual**

Flowers: White, pink, coral, red, and bicolored single or double (Ø 1–2 in [2–5 cm]). **Soil:** Well-drained, evenly moist, rich, soil amended with lots of peat, leaf mold, or compost.
Care: Tiny seeds can be difficult to start. Best to purchase trans plants and set out after danger of frost has passed. Mulch and lightly fertilize plants after setting out in the garden. Keep plants well watered. **Design:** Best used as edgings or massed in beds and borders. An unbeatable plant for container plantings.

Fleabane
Erigeron hybrids
Height/Width: 20–32 in (50–80 cm)/ 12–16 in (30–40 cm)
Blooms: June–July (Sept.)
Perennial

► **popular companion perennial**

Flowers: White, pink, violet, and lavender with golden eye (Ø 2¹/₂ in [6 cm]). **Soil:** Fresh, nutrient-rich, well-drained, not too heavy. **Care:** Water during dry spells; support if necessary; cut off spent flowers; after flowering cut back by one-third and fertilize with compost, which promotes a second flowering in September; every few years divide in fall or spring. **Design:** Very beautiful in color-coordinated groups in a bed; also a pretty cut flower when in full bloom. **Zone:** 2–9.

EXPERT TIP
Recommended hybrids: 'Dragon Wings' is excellent for hanging baskets.

EXPERT TIP
The variety pictured is 'Summer Snow'.

Rewarding Summer Flowers

Perennial Phlox

Phlox paniculata hybrids
Height/Width: 20–59 in (50–150 cm)/ up to 20 in (50 cm)
Blooms: June–September
Perennial

▶ **lavish flower display**

Flowers: White, pink, red, crimson, violet, often bicolored with pink or white eyes (Ø 1/2 in [1.5 cm]). **Soil:** Fresh to moist, but well-drained and no standing water; nutrient- and humus-rich. **Care:** Shallow rooted and so wilts easily; therefore water regularly; in spring provide with organic fertilizer or compost; support tall varieties; in severe climates provide winter protection with compost or leaves. **Design:** Ideal for borders and beds; plant color-coordinated varieties in groups. **Zone:** 3–9.

Hosta

Hosta species and hybrids
Height/Width: 4–47 in (10–120 cm)/ 12–39 in (30–100 cm)
Blooms: June–August
Perennial

▶ **growth form and leaves are attractive**

Flowers: White, light violet to lavender-blue and purple (Ø 1/2 in [1.5–2 cm]). **Soil:** Loamy, even damp is all right, containing much humus. **Care:** In spring provide with organic fertilizer or compost as mulch; combat snails when growth starts; otherwise trouble free; propagation by division possible after flowering. **Design:** For edges of woods and pools; for shady perennial beds as a permanent focal point; best suited for covering bulbs as they go dormant. **Zone:** 4–8.

Lupine

Lupinus polyphyllus hybrids
Height/Width: 32–39 in (80–100 cm)/ 20–24 in (50–60 cm)
Blooms: June–July
Perennial

▶ **plants with much charm**

Flowers: White, yellow, orange, pink, red, violet, blue, also bicolors (Ø 1/4–1/2 in [1–2 cm]), inflorescences 16–20-in [40–50-cm] -tall). **Soil:** Moderately dry to fresh, well-drained, sandy, moderately rich, no alkaline soil. **Care:** Provide with compost in spring; after flowering, cut back main flower stalk to younger side shoots; leave the leaves. **Design:** Ideal for the background of the bed; best effects in mixed-color groups. **Zone:** 3/4–9.

EXPERT TIP
The varieties pictured are 'Rosa Pastell' and 'Flamingo'.

EXPERT TIP
The variety pictured is 'The Chatelaine'.

**After the bulbs have finished,
fill in the gaps with annuals or perennials
that leaf out later, such as hosta.**

Mealy-cup Sage

Salvia farinacea
Height/Width: 20–32 in (50–80 cm)/
12–16 in (30–40 cm)
Blooms: June–October
Annual in culture

▶ **trouble-free long bloomer**

Flowers: Silver-white, blue, dark blue, violet (Ø $1/2$ in [1 cm]). **Soil:** Fresh, loose, nutrient-rich, slightly alkaline, not soggy. **Care:** Sow from April to May directly in the bed; planting after last chance of frost; prepare bed well first with compost or organic fertilizer; water regularly. Can be grown as a perennial in warmer areas. **Design:** Showy bedding plant; place in groups; very beautiful with red roses or yellow border perennials; also suitable flower for cutting. **Zone:** 6/7–9.

Marigold

Tagetes patula hybrids, shown: 'Bolero'
Height/Width: 8–20 in (20–50 cm)/
8–12 in (20–30 cm)
Blooms: June–October
Annual

▶ **trouble-free and excellent bloomer**

Flowers: Yellow, orange, red-brown, also bicolors, single, semidouble, and double, strongly scented (Ø 1–$1^1/2$ in [3–4 cm]). **Soil:** Damp to moderately dry, all normal garden soils, also moist. **Care:** Sow in bed from May, planting after all danger of frost is past; prepare soil with compost or organic fertilizer; keep moderately damp; cut off spent flowers. **Design:** In beds or borders, arrange double varieties in groups, single varieties in ribbons or carpets; also for container plants; good flowers for cutting.

Impatiens

Impatiens wallerana
Height/Width: 8–20 in (20–50 cm)/
12–30 in (30–71 cm)
Blooms: April–October
Annual

▶ **favorite bedding plant for shade**

Flowers: Pink, purple, red, orange, salmon, light blue, and white (Ø 1–$2^1/2$ in [2–6 cm]) dainty single and double flowers. **Soil:** Moist, well-drained soil. Lightly fertilize and mulch plants after planting. **Care:** Start seeds indoors 10–12 weeks before the last frost or buy transplants to set out after last chance of frost; pinch back for a bushier habit. **Design:** Best used massed in shady beds, borders, or as edgings and groundcover under trees; excellent plant for hanging baskets, window boxes, and containers.

GOOD PARTNERS
*Almost all annuals,
helenium, rudbeckia*

EXPERT TIP
*'Rose Parade' and 'Rosette Mix' are
gorgeous double-flowered hybrids.*

Glorious Color in Midsummer

Plants for Sunny Locations

Name	Flower Color Flowering Time	Height (in/cm) Type
Agapanthus hybrids Lily-of-the-Nile	blue, white July–August	12–35 (30–90) perennial
Centranthus ruber Jupiter's Beard	pink, white June–September	20–28 (50–70) perennial
Coreopsis verticillata Tickseed	golden yellow June–September	12–28 (30–70) perennial
Echinacea purpurea Coneflower	pink, red, white July–September	28–39 (70–100) perennial
Echinops bannaticus Globe thistle	silvery blue July–September	32–55 (80–140) perennial
Helianthemum hybrids Sunrose	white, orange, red June–September	6–12 (15–30) perennial
Kniphofia hybrids Red-hot poker	yellow, orange, red June–September	24–55 (60–140) perennial
Lavatera trimestris Tree mallow	white, pink, red July–September	20–32 (50–80) annual
Liatris spicata Gayfeather	violet, white, red July–September	16–35 (40–90) perennial
Platycodon grandiflorus Balloon flower	blue, white, pink July–August	8–28 (20–70) perennial
Solidago hybrids Goldenrod	blue, white, pink July–August	20–32 (50–80) perennial
Veronica spicata ssp. *incana*, Silver speedwell	dark-blue June–August	8–20 (20–50) perennial

Plants for Part Shade

Aconitum napellus Monkshood	blue, white, pink June–August	35–59 (90–150) perennial
Astrantia major Masterwort	white, pink, red June–August	20–28 (50–70) perennial
Centaurea montana Cornflower	blue, white, pink May–July	16–20 (40–50) perennial
Chelone obliqua Turtlehead	pink July–September	20–32 (50–80) perennial
Euphorbia griffithii Spurge	orange-red May–June	20–32 (50–80) perennial
Geranium sylvaticum Cranesbill	violet, white, blue May–July	12–24 (30–60) perennial
Heuchera hybrids Coral bells	white, pink, red May–July	16–28 (40–70) perennial
Lysimachia punctata Yellow loosestrife	golden yellow June–September	32–47 (80–120) perennial
Lobelia cardinalis Cardinal flower	red July–September	24–46 (60–90) perennial

Allium
Allium giganteum
Height/Width: 32–59 in (80–150 cm)/ 10–12 in (25–30 cm)
Blooms: June–July
Bulb

► **striking inflorescence**

Flowers: Reddish violet (tiny flowers cover large globe-shaped flower heads Ø 8 in [20 cm] on sturdy stems).
Soil: Dry, also fresh, well-drained, warm; thrives also on poor soils, but grows shorter there. **Care:** Plant bulbs in fall; fertilize with organic fertilizer about every 2 years; if no seeds are wanted, cut off spent flowers. **Design:** Especially beautiful in borders in small groups together with other, lower ornamental onion species. **Zone:** 4–9.

Hollyhocks
Alcea rosea
Height/Width: 63–87 in (160–220 cm)/ 16–24 in (40-60 cm)
Blooms: July–September
Annual or biennial in culture

► **classic cottage garden plant**

Flowers: White, yellow, pink, crimson, red to blackish-red, single and double (Ø $2^1/_2$–3 in [6–8 cm]).
Soil: Moderately dry to fresh, well-drained, deeply cultivated, nutrient-rich. **Care:** Sow April–May (annual culture) or June–July (biennial culture); fertilize the soil heavily with organic fertilizer, mulch well; stake. **Design:** Especially beautiful along a house wall or a fence, in small, color-coordinated groups or individually as a tall focal point. **Zone:** 4–8.

GOOD PARTNERS
Nepeta, peonies, cranesbill

**"Tame" the utterly boundless wealth
of summer flower choices by limiting
your garden to one or a few basic colors.**

Shasta Daisy
Leucanthemum maximum
Height/Width: 20–35 in (50–90 cm)/
12–20 in (30–50 cm)
Blooms: June–September
Perennial

▶ **looks natural, is robust**

Flowers: White with yellow center,
depending on variety, single, double,
or semidouble (Ø about 2–2¹/₂ in [5–6
cm]). **Soil:** Fresh to moderately dry,
nutrient-rich, loose, any garden soil,
only not too sandy or clayish. **Care:**
Fertilize with organic fertilizer in
spring; water during dry spells; remove
spent flowers; cut back hard after
flowering and fertilize with compost
for second flowering in late summer;
every 3–4 years divide in spring.
Design: Place in groups in the summer
bed; the white of the flowers combines
with almost all colors. **Zone:** 5–9.

Astilbe
Astilbe arendsii hybrids
Height/Width: 24–47 in (60–120 cm)/
20–32 in (50–80 cm)
Blooms: July–September
Perennial

▶ **ideal for semishady places**

Flowers: Depending on variety white,
pink, red, lavender (individual flowers
tiny; they are clustered in large,
plume-like inflorescences). **Soil:**
Loamy, rich in humus, moist; other
conditions are tolerated, but will not
tolerate hot and dry conditions. **Care:**
Apply organic fertilizer in the spring
and mulch with compost; water regularly; cut off faded flowers; in severe
climates cover with leaves before first
frost. **Design:** Along the edges of
wooded areas and in beds, combine
varieties with different flowering
times and colors. **Zone:** 4–8.

Black Cohosh, Black Snakeroot
Cimicifuga racemosa
Height/Width: 59–79 in (150–200 cm)/
20–35 in (50–90 cm)
Blooms: July–August
Perennial

▶ **striking and long-lived**

Flowers: White (tiny individual flowers
in 24-in- [60-cm-] long candle-like
inflorescences). **Soil:** Loose, moist,
rich in humus, under no circumstances
dry soil. Will grow in full sun if soil is
kept moist. **Care:** Fertilize in spring
with compost; water regularly, especially during dry spells; don't dig or
transplant, as they develop best
when left undisturbed. **Design:** Very
beautiful in front of a dark background; use cimicifuga in groups
in front of wooded areas or in the
shadow of a wall. Does best in
cooler areas. **Zone:** 3–9.

EXPERT TIP
Pictured is the variety 'Wirral Pride'.

GOOD PARTNERS
Hosta, evergreens, astilbe

Vigorous Midsummer Bloomers

Bee Balm

Monarda hybrids, shown: 'Mohawk'
Height/Width: 28–51 in (70–130 cm)/
8–20 in (20–50 cm)
Blooms: July–September
Perennial

▶ **fragrant foliage**

Flowers: Pink, almost all shades of
red, violet, and white, very aromatically fragrant (Ø 2–2³/₄ in [5–7 cm]).
Soil: Fresh to moist, nutrient-rich,
loose and humous; heavy soils not
suitable. **Care:** Fertilize in spring
with compost or rotted manure;
water thoroughly during dry spells;
support tall varieties; cut back in
fall; if flowering diminishes, divide
in spring or fall and replant in fresh
soil. **Design:** In groups in the middle
as a focal point, also for the edge of
a wooded area. **Zone:** 4–9.

Catmint

Nepeta x *faassenii*, shown: 'Walker's Low'
Height/Width: 12–20 (30–50 cm)/
16–20 in (40–50 cm)
Blooms: May–September
Perennial

▶ **long-lasting flowers**

Flowers: Lavender- to lilac-blue (Ø
8 mm, inflorescences an inch or so
[several cm] high). **Soil:** Any normal
garden soil that isn't too heavy;
dry soils are tolerated; well-drained;
no winter wetness. **Care:** Fertilize
sparingly; cut back after flowering,
which leads to compact growth and
reblooming in fall; on moderately
heavy soil, protect from water in
winter by covering. **Design:** Good
companion for roses; also beautiful
in a border combined with strongly
colored perennials. **Zone:** 4–8.

Tobacco Plant

Nicotiana sylvestris
Height/Width: 39–59 in (100–150 cm)/
8–12 in (20–30 cm)
Blooms: June–October
Annual

▶ **very decorative**

Flowers: White, fragrant (Ø 5 mm,
¹/₄–¹/₂ in [1–2 cm] long). **Soil:**
Fresh, moderately heavy, loose,
nutrient rich. **Care:** Sow indoors in
March or set purchased plants out
after last danger of frost; prepare
soil well with compost; water during
dry spells; cut off spent flowers.
Design: Very beautiful together
with its near relative *Nicotiana alata*,
which comes with white, yellow,
pink, red, and violet flowers, in the
center of beds; low-growing varieties
suitable for container culture.

GOOD PARTNERS
Fleabane, campanulas,
grasses, baby's-breath

GOOD PARTNERS
Asters, delphiniums, cosmos

**In this group you will also find tall perennials
that you can plant like bouquets between
lower ones or in lush, mixed groups.**

Zinnia
Zinnia elegans
Height/Width: 12–39 in (30–100 cm)/
6–12 in (15–30 cm)
Blooms: July–October
Annual

▶ **many wonderfully colored varieties**

Flowers: White, yellow, orange, pink,
red, violet, also bicolors, small- and
large-flowered, single to doubled into
pompoms (Ø an inch or so [several
cm]). Zinnias range from 1–5 inches
with a variety of colors and shapes.
Soil: Somewhat damp, rich, well-
drained. **Care:** Sow indoors in April or
put out bought plants after last frost;
protect seedlings and young plants
from snails and slugs; add compost
to the soil; stake tall varieties; deadhead. **Design:** Beautiful in the bed in
groups; low varieties as edging; also
for containers.

Regal Lily, Royal Lily
Lilium regale
Height/Width: 24–59 in (60–150 cm)/
12 in (30 cm)
Blooms: July
Bulb

▶ **magnificent, noble flowers**

Flowers: White with yellow throat;
outside pink striped; also pure-white
varieties; heavily fragrant (Ø about
2 1/2 in [6 cm]). **Soil:** Fresh, well-
drained, nutrient-rich, humusy, also
alkaline. **Care:** Plant bulbs in fall if
possible; in winter cover with mulch;
fertilize well with rotted compost
when growth starts; water in dry
spells during growing season; discreetly support long stems; cut off
spent flowers. **Design:** Very beautiful
in groups of two to three between
lower perennials or in the cottage
garden. **Zone:** 4–9.

Black-eyed Susan
Rudbeckia species
Height/Width: 20–79 in (50–200 cm)/
20–39 in (50–100 cm)
Blooms: July–September
Perennial

▶ **abundant long-lived flowers**

Flowers: Yellow, usually with a
darker center, single and double—
pictured is *R. fulgida* var. *sullivantii*
'Goldsturm' (Ø 2 1/2 in [6 cm]).
Soil: Good garden soil, loose,
nutrient-rich, fresh, loamy. **Care:** In
spring, fertilize with compost or
well-rotted manure; water thoroughly
during dry spells; stake tall species
and varieties; remove spent flowers.
Design: In perennial borders in
which strong colors predominate;
also along a fence, which supports
them unobtrusively. **Zone:** 4–9.

EXPERT TIP
The variety Z. angustifolia *grows to
only 8–20 in (20–50 cm) high.*

EXPERT TIP
*There are many other lily
species, also for part shade.*

Dahlias and Gladiolas

Single Dahlias

Variety Group	Flower Color Of special note	Height (in/cm) Flower size (in/cm)
'Andrea' Dwarf single dahlia	yellow yellow center	8–12/20–30 $1/2$–$1^1/2$/2–4
'Rosa Zwerg' Dwarf single dahlia	red yellow center	8/20 $1/2$–$1^1/2$/2–4
'Anna Karina' Single dahlia	white yellow center	16/40 2–4/5–10
'Roxy' Single dahlia	wine-red dark foliage	16/40 2–4/5–10
'Gartenparty' Tall single dahlia	yellow-orange yellow center	24/60 2–4/5–10
'Park Princess' Tall single dahlia	pink yellow center	24/60 2–4/5–10

Semidouble Dahlias

'Bishop of Llandaff' Peony-flowered dahlias	fire-red dark foliage	39/100 3–6/8–15
'Olympic Fire' Peony-flowered dahlias	orange-red dark foliage	43/110 3–6/8–15
'Cricket' Collarette dahlias	red and yellow bicolored	35/90 $2^3/4$–5/7–12
'Rondo' Collarette dahlias	lavender and white bicolored	43/110 $2^3/4$–5/7–12
'Comet' Anemone-flowered dahlias	chestnut-brown raised center	32–39/80–100 $2^3/4$–5/7–12
'Monsieur Dupont' Anemone-flowered dahlias	purplish pink raised center	32/80 $2^3/4$–5/7–12

Double Dahlias

'Golden Horn' Cactus dahlia	orange tubular petals	32/80 over 6/15
'Marianne Strauss' Cactus dahlia	purplish pink tubular petals	43/110 over 6/15
'Mairo' Formal decorative dahlia	violet densely doubled	39/100 over 6/15
'White Label' Formal decorative dahlia	white densely doubled	39–47/100–120 over 6/15
'Annette' Ball dahlia	pink globular flower	47/120 4/10
'Robin Hood' Ball dahlia	orange-red dark foliage	32–39/80–100 4/10
'Robina' Pompon dahlia	ruby-red globular flower	39/100 2/5
'Snowflake' Pompon dahlia	white globular flower	39/100 2/5

Sword Lily

Gladiolus hybrids, shown: 'Charme'
Height/Width: 16–55 in (40–140 cm)/
8–12 in (20–30 cm)
Blooms: June–September
Corm, not winter-hardy

Flowers: All colors except blue and black, also bi- and multicolored (Ø up to 6 in [15 cm], 16–20-in [40–50-cm] -tall inflorescence). **Soil:** Fresh to slightly damp, deeply cultivated, well-drained, nutrient-rich. **Care:** Plant corms in May, cover shoots against late frosts; water during dry spells; support tall varieties; remove end of October and store in a frost-free place. **Design:** Very beautiful in small groups as a visual accent in the background of the bed and along a fence. **Zone:** Perennial in zones 9–11 only.

Formal Decorative Dahlia

Dahlia hybrids, shown: 'Purple Joy'
Height/Width: 32–59 in (80–150 cm)/
20–32 in (50–80 cm)
Blooms: June–October
Tuber, not winter-hardy

Flowers: Densely doubled, curving rayed flowers; all colors except blue and black, also multicolors (Ø to over 4 in [10 cm]). **Soil:** Slightly damp, well-drained, nutrient-rich, moderately heavy, humusy. **Care:** Plant tubers from the end of April; add potassium fertilizer; support tall varieties; cut back after the first frost, dig out tubers, and winter in a frost-free place. **Design:** Combine with color-coordinated gladiolus or other dahlias in the bed. **Zone:** Perennial in zones 9–11 only.

EXPERT TIP
*Many hybrid varieties
of varying sizes*

If you keep removing faded flowers, dahlias will bloom from summer until the first frost. Don't forget to lift tubers out of the soil and store indoors over the winter in a cool but frost-free place.

Single Dahlia

Dahlia hybrids, shown: 'Fellbacher Gold'
Height/Width: 12–16 in (30–40 cm)/ 12–16 in (30–40 cm)
Blooms: July–October
Tuber, not winter-hardy

▶ **they create a very natural effect**

Flowers: Single wreath of rayed petals, all colors except blue and black; many shades of yellow and red (Ø about 2^1/$_2$ in [6 cm]).
Soil: Slightly damp, well-drained, nutrient-rich, moderately heavy, humusy. **Care:** Plant tubers from end of April; apply potassium fertilizer; protect from late frosts; water during dry spells; stake tall varieties; cut back after first frost, dig out tubers, and winter over free from frost.
Design: Beautiful in a flower bed with single-flowered annuals; low-growing varieties also in containers.

Collarette Dahlia

Dahlia hybrids, shown: 'Grand Duc'
Height/Width: 28–39 in (70–100 cm)/ 20–32 in (50–80 cm)
Blooms: June–October
Tuber, not winter-hardy

▶ **especially good for combinations**

Flowers: Semidouble, outer rosette of broad petals, in the center more delicate rayed flowers, usually a different color; all colors except blue and black (Ø 2^3/$_4$–5 in [7–12 cm]).
Soil: Fresh, well-drained, nutrient-rich, moderately heavy, humusy.
Care: Plant corms from the end of April; fertilize with potassium; protect from late frosts; water during dry spells; cut back after the first frost, dig out tubers, and winter over frost free. **Design:** Good in combination with many perennials.

Cactus Dahlia

Dahlia hybrids, shown: 'Valhalla'
Height/Width: 32–39 in (80–100 cm)/ 20–28 in (50–70 cm)
Blooms: June–October
Tuber, not winter-hardy

▶ **very striking flowers**

Flowers: Densely doubled, tubular rayed flowers, all colors except blue and black (Ø 4–10 in [10–25 cm]).
Soil: Fresh, well-drained, nutrient-rich, moderately heavy, humusy.
Care: Plant tubers from end of April; fertilize with potassium; protect from late frosts; water during dry spells; stake high varieties; cut back after the first frost, dig out tubers, and winter over in a frost-free place.
Design: Especially beautiful in the center of the perennial bed; coordinate colors well.

GOOD PARTNERS
Speedwell, marguerite, delphinium, sage

GOOD PARTNERS
Grasses, daisies, sage, cosmos

EXPERT TIP
Semicactus dahlias have semitubular-rayed flowers.

Flowers with the Charm of Wild Plants

Lady's-mantle
Alchemilla mollis
Height/Width: 12–20 in (30–50 cm)/
16–24 in (40–60 cm)
Blooms: June–August
Wild perennial

▶ **can be combined in a number of ways, robust**

Flowers: Greenish-yellow, a particularly strong-growing and large-flowered garden variety (Ø inflorescence 2–3 in [5–8 cm]). **Soil:** Nutrient-rich, if possible loamy or clayish, fresh, not too sandy. **Care:** Remove dead foliage in March; fertilize when new growth appears; remove spent flowers; cutting back after flowering leads to new flowering in September. **Design:** Provides an oasis of quiet in colorful beds, good contrast with red, calm with blue flowers. **Zone:** 4–7.

Greater Bellflower
Campanula latifolia var. *macrantha*
Height/Width: 32–39 in (80–100 cm)/
20–24 in (50–60 cm)
Blooms: June–July
Perennial

▶ **robust and easy-care**

Flowers: Blue-violet, a pure-white variety (Ø 1–1¹/₂ in [3–4 cm]). **Soil:** Fresh to moist, also tolerates damp soils, nutrient-rich, humusy, well-drained. **Care:** Use organic fertilizer in spring, preferably with decayed cow manure; protect new growth from slugs; water during dry spells; mulch in fall. **Design:** Very beautiful in light shade of woody plants or along the edge of woods with other forest plants; also in partly shaded perennial beds and in natural gardens.

Purple Coneflower
Echinacea purpurea
Height/Width: 3–4 ft (90–120 cm)/
4 ft (120 cm)
Blooms: July–September
Perennial

▶ **trouble-free and adaptable**

Flowers: Large, striking pink to purple daisy-like flowers with prominent iridescent rusty orange central "cones." **Soil:** Prefers a well-drained, loamy soil but will grow in poor, dry, heavier soil. **Care:** Start plants from seed or divide established plantings in spring or fall; cut back in either late fall or early spring; tolerates heat and drought well. **Design:** Excellent for middle to back of borders, informal, more naturalized plantings, and meadows; excellent plant for butterfly gardens; long lasting cut flowers and cones can be used for dried arrangements. **Zone:** 3–9.

GOOD PARTNERS
Sweet Williams, delphinium, campanulas

GOOD PARTNERS
Ferns, hosta, cimicifuga, goatsbeard

EXPERT TIP
'Bright Star' is an attractive maroon-colored cultivar.

The shapes of plants and flowers help determine the character of a bed. When you use natural-looking plants, your garden gains a natural appearance.

Meadow Sage

Salvia x superba, shown: 'Blue Hill'
Height/Width: 16–32 in (40–80 cm)/
12–16 in (30–40 cm)
Blooms: May–August
Perennial

▶ **in flower for a long time**

Flowers: Light to dark violet-blue, fragrant (Ø 5 mm, in long spikes about 8 in [20 cm] long). **Soil:** Moderately dry to fresh, well-drained, nutrient rich; the species tolerates dry soil; heavy soils unsuitable. **Care:** Apply organic fertilizer when first growth appears; remove spent flowers; cut back hard after flowering and fertilize with compost, which will lead to flowering again in September. **Design:** Place in perennial beds for contrast with yellow- and red-flowered plants; also for rose beds and cottage gardens. **Zone:** 5–9.

Rodgersia

Rodgersia podophylla
Height/Width: 32–39 in (80–100 cm)/
24–30 in (60 75 cm)
Blooms: June–July
Perennial

▶ **leaf interest for shade**

Flowers: Creamy white (Ø a few mm, in panicles up to 20 in [50 cm] long). **Soil:** Fresh to damp, well-drained, nutrient-rich, containing humus, well-aerated, no wet or compacted soils. **Care:** Remove dead plant parts in spring, provide with compost or combined organic-chemical fertilizer when growth starts; water abundantly during dry spells. **Design:** Ideal along the edges of ponds or under shrubs; the large leaves make an effective contrast of shapes and, depending on the variety, turn dark red in fall. **Zone:** 5–8.

Silver Speedwell

Veronica spicata ssp. *incana*
Height/Width: 8–16 in [20–40 cm]/
8–16 in [20–40]
Blooms: June–August
Perennial

▶ **valuable ornamental foliage plant**

Flowers: Dark-blue or deep violet; create beautiful contrast to the silver-gray leaves (individual flowers a few mm, in spikes 6 in [15 cm] long). **Soil:** Moderately dry to fresh, well-drained, moderately rich, also stony or sandy. **Care:** Fertilize with good mature compost when new growth starts; remove spent flowers regularly. **Design:** The gray foliage harmonizes in beds and borders outstandingly with pastel-colored perennials and red roses; also for the rock and heather garden. **Zone:** 4–8.

GOOD PARTNERS
Bearded iris, fleabane, peonies, roses

EXPERT TIP
Other gray-leaved plants: pinks, artemisia, lamb's ears.

Fall Flowers

These plants only really get going long after the fireworks of the other flowers have fizzled out. With careful choice, the fall bloomers prolong the growing season until the first heavy frost.

In the fall the garden slowly grows more tranquil. Less often do daytime temperatures invite spending several hours on the terrace. Yet the garden still has much to offer at this time of year: If you have deadheaded your summer flowers regularly, some will now form buds once again—if not so lavishly as during their chief flowering season.

But the real fall bloomers are just now coming into their own. During the summer you saw only their foliage between the other flowers; now they are next up.

Proper Planning

When planning your bed, make sure that you group the fall bloomers for best effect. Then it isn't just a matter of some flowers sparkling here and there—you see compact areas of color, which also make an autumn bed a feast for the eyes. A good

plan is especially important when it comes to fall gardens: Whereas the blossoms of the summer flowers contributed to the dominant overall impression earlier, it is now their growth forms that take on a not inconsiderable role. Make the effort to entirely remove all the stems of the finished flowers, so that now only the fall flowers appear above the various shades of green and different-shaped leaves.

If you are not content with the look of the bed, however, you can use a simple trick: Buy some more containers of ready-grown flowering plants and set them in shallow dishes. These go in between the other plants in the middle of the garden, preferably so that the containers don't show. You can also liven up the fall beds with appropriate colored garden accessories, like garden globes.

Fall comes to the garden with warm golden colors.

Glowing Early Fall

Fall Bloomers for Sunny Places

Plant Name	Flower Color Of Special Note	Height (in/cm) When Flowers
Anaphalis triplinervis Pearl Everlasting	silvery-white gray foliage	8–20/20–50 July–Sept
Artemisia abrotanum Southernwood	yellow-green silvery foliage	32–39/80–100 July–Oct
Crocosmia x crocosmiiflora Montbretia	yellow, orange, red needs winter care	20–32/50–80 July–Sept
Crocus kotschyanus Autumn Crocus	pinky purple yellow center	4/10 Sept–Oct
Crocus medius Autumn Crocus	dark lilac yellow center	23/4–4/7–10 Oct–Nov
Dendranthema arcticum Arctic Daisy	white, yellow, pink creeping	10–16/25–40 Sept–Oct
Eupatorium maculatum Joe-Pye Weed	crimson yellow fall color	59–79/150–200 Aug–Oct
Gentiana asclepiadea Gentian	white, dark-blue trumpet flowers	8–24/20–60 July–Oct
Leucanthemella serotina Field or Oxeye Daisy	white many flowers	51–63/130–160 Sept–Oct
Leucojum autumnale Autumn Snowflake	white poisonous	4–8/10–20 Sept–Oct

Fall Bloomers for Part Shade

Anemone japonica Japanese Anemone	light- to dark-rose single flowers	24–32/60–80 Aug–Sept
Cimicifuga simplex Bugbane	white fragrant	39–59/100–150 Sept–Oct
Colchicum autumnale Autmn Crcus, Mdw Sffrn	white, pink, lilac also double, poisonous	4–6/10–15 Sept–Oct
Colchicum byzantinum	lilac pink full flowers, poisonous	6–8/15–20 Aug–Sept
Colchicum hybrids	pink, lilac, violet poisonous	4–6/10–15 Aug–Oct
Cyclamen cilicium Fall-flowering Cyclamen	light violet-blue frost-tender	8/20 Sept–Oct
Gentiana sinoornata Gentian	deep azure blue striped w/purple-blue	4–6/10–15 Sept–Nov
Hosta tardiflora Plantain Lily	light violet olive-green leaves	8–12/20–30 Sept–Nov
Saxifraga cortusifolia var. *fortunei*, Saxifrage	white won't tolerate lime	18/45 Sept–Oct
Sedum spectabile Stonecrop	pink to purple gray-green leaves	12–16/30–40 Aug–Sept
Silene schafta Campion, Catchfly	white, pink cushion plant	4–8/10–20 Aug–Sept

Chrysanthemums
Dendranthema grandiflorum hybrids
Height/Width: 16–39 [40–100]/ 24 in [60 cm]
Blooms: August–November
Perennial

▶ **very large choice of varieties**

Flowers: All colors except blue and violet; single, semidouble, double, ball-shaped (Ø very diverse). **Soil:** Moderately dry to fresh, well-drained, loose, not too clayish, rich, also alkaline. **Care:** Fertilize with rotted manure or compost when new growth appears; support tall species at flowering time; cover with brush in late fall; fallen leaves are less suitable since fungus can spread underneath. **Design:** Very beautiful in sunny spots in front of woods with fall coloring and in front of warm walls. **Zone:** 4–9.

Cosmos
Cosmos bipinnatus
Height/Width: 20–43 in (50–110 cm)/ 20–24 in (50–60 cm)
Blooms: June–October
Annual

▶ **large flowers and feathery leaves**

Flowers: White, pink, red to crimson, yellow center (Ø about 2 in [5 cm]). **Soil:** Fresh, well-drained, loose, nutrient-rich. **Care:** Sow from March to April directly into the bed; furnish soil with plenty of compost before sowing or planting; water well during dry periods; stake tall varieties; deadhead regularly. **Design:** Wonderful for cottage gardens; beautiful in small groups in the perennial bed, in front of walls or fences, also in containers; good cut flower.

EXPERT TIP
Illustrated is the early-blooming variety 'Anastasia'.

GOOD PARTNERS
Asters, bee balm, phlox, cleome

In early fall, cut back the spent summer flowers so they don't spoil the effect of the fall flowers.

Obedience Plant
Physostegia virginiana, shown: 'Vivid'
Height/Width: 24–47 in (60–120 cm)/ 20–24 in (50–60 cm)
Blooms: July–September
Perennial

▶ **full spikes**

Flowers: White, pink to light-violet red (Ø about ¹/₄ in [1 cm]). **Soil:** Fresh, also tolerates damp soils, nutrient-rich, humusy, somewhat loamy. **Care:** Supply well with compost in spring; water plentifully during dry spells; stake high varieties; cut back in fall; divide very large clumps; in harsh locations cover with branches for protection from frost. **Design:** Very beautiful along the edges of ponds or streams; also an imporant fall bloomer for the perennial bed; cut flowers last a long time. **Zone:** 3–9.

Verbena
Verbena hybrids, shown: 'Novalis'
Height/Width: 8–16 in (20–40 cm)/ 8–16 in (20–40 cm)
Blooms: June–September
Annual

▶ **flowers lushly and long**

Flowers: White, pink, salmon, red, blue, violet, often with white eye, also bicolored (Ø about ¹/₂ in [1 cm]). **Soil:** Fresh to moderately dry, well-drained, no standing water, rich, humusy. **Care:** Sowing indoors in early spring is possible but not easy, since verbena seeds must be chilled before sowing (put presoaked seed in the refrigerator for several days); set out plants in the garden after all danger of frost; water during dry spells; remove spent flowers. **Design:** Put in small clusters in the bed; also very beautiful in containers.

Snapdragons
Antirrhinum majus
Height/Width: 8–47 in (20–120 cm)/ 6–18 in (15–45 cm)
Blooms: June–September
Annual

▶ **splendid colors and long-flowering**

Flowers: White, yellow, golden-yellow, bronze, copper-orange, red-orange, pink, dark-red (Ø ¹/₂–1 in [1–3 cm]). **Soil:** Normal garden soil, loose, rich. **Care:** Sow indoors in early spring; put out self-sown or bought plants after last frost in garden soil amended with compost; tolerates light late frost; water moderately; stake tall varieties; regularly cut off spent flowers. **Design:** Beautiful in mixed colors in the border, tall varieties in the background, medium-tall in the middle, dwarf varieties at the edge, or raise in planters.

GOOD PARTNERS
Grasses, cosmos, cleome

EXPERT TIP
Combine varieties of different heights.

The Flowers of Fall

Mountain Fleece
Polygonum amplexicaule
Height/Width: 32–47 in (80–120 cm)/ 30 in (70 cm)
Blooms: August–October
Perennial

▶ **ideal in wet spots**

Flowers: White, fire-red, ruby red (individual flowers tiny, but inflorescence 4–6 in [10–15 cm] long). **Soil:** Fresh to moist, also tolerates damp soil well; rich in nutrients and humus. **Care:** Provide compost regularly; water abundantly during dry spells or the leaves will turn brown; cut back in late fall; when spreads too much, simply cut off the unwanted plants with the spade. **Design:** Very beautiful as an edging plant around a pond, in the background of borders, and along the edges of woods. **Zone:** 5–9.

Japanese Anemone
Anemone japonica hybrids
Height/Width: 24–55 in (60–140 cm)/ 24–39 in (60–100 cm)
Blooms: August–October
Perennial

▶ **important for fall beds**

Flowers: White, pale pink, pure pink, violet pink, crimson, dark-red, single and semidouble (Ø about 2 in [5 cm]). **Soil:** Fresh to moist, wet soils are tolerated, loose, rich in humus and nutrients. **Care:** Above all, water during dry spells; fertilize with compost or rotted manure; mulch in fall; with frost cover with leaves or branches. **Design:** Beautiful along the edges of woods or in the shady areas of beds. **Zone:** 5–8.

Sedum, Stonecrop
Sedum telephium hybrids
Height/Width: 12–24 in (30–60 cm)/ up to 24 in (60 cm)
Blooms: August–September
Perennial

▶ **many subspecies, robust**

Flowers: Depending on subspecies and variety, purple to brownish red (individual flowers tiny, arching umbrella of a flower up to 12 in [30 cm] wide). **Soil:** Dry to fresh; dry soils are tolerated well; well-drained; possibly with a high sand or gravel content. **Care:** Amend heavy soils with sand before planting; fertilize with organic fertilizer only every 3–4 years; otherwise leave undisturbed; the brownish red seed heads remain attractive for a long time; only cut them back in spring. **Design:** Ideal for rock gardens and dry beds. **Zone:** 3/4–9.

EXPERT TIP
Pictured is the variety 'Honorine Jobert'.

EXPERT TIP
Pictured is the variety 'Autumn Joy'.

Shade-tolerant fall flowers need not necessarily grow in flower beds. They create their effects just as well in front of the colored foliage of shrubs.

Azure Monkshood
Aconitum carmichaelii var. *wilsonii*
Height/Width: 39–55 in (100–140 cm)/ about 16 in (40 cm)
Blooms: September–October
Perennial

▶ **striking inflorescences**

Flowers: Blue to violet (Ø ¹/₄–¹/₂ in [1–2 cm], in inflorescences up to 12 in [30 cm] long). **Soil:** Sufficiently moist, rich in nutrients, humus. **Care:** Fertilize heavily with organic fertilizer in spring, preferably with bone meal or well-rotted manure; cut back to the ground after flowering, wearing gloves while doing so as protection from the poisonous plant juices. **Design:** Most beautiful along the edges of wooded areas and in the natural garden, also for not very sunny beds. **Zone:** 4–8.

Toad Lily
Tricyrtis hirta
Height/Width: 20–35 in (50–90 cm)/ 16–24 in (40 60 cm)
Blooms: September–October
Perennial

▶ **very attractive, somewhat delicate**

Flowers: Orchid-like, star shaped, white to yellow background with purplish-violet to lilac spots (Ø 2 in [5 cm]). **Soil:** Fresh to moist, well-drained, very rich in humus, acid to neutral. **Care:** Mulch soil with leaf compost; water during dry spells and provide high humidity with sprinkling; cover with leaves to protect from frost. **Design:** Use as a special focal point under light woody plants and along the cool edge of wooded areas, but don't put next to any vigorous partners. **Zone:** 4–9.

Fall-flowering Crocus
Crocus speciosus
Height/Width: 4–6 in (10–15 cm)/ 2–4 in (5–10 cm)
Blooms: September–November
Bulb

▶ **very natural effect**

Flowers: White, lavender, violet-blue, some dark-veined, and with a light throat (Ø about 1¹/₄ in [4 cm]). **Soil:** Fresh, well-drained. **Care:** Plant September-November; apply organic fertilizer every few years in the fall; let foliage die back after flowering; mulch. **Design:** Like spring-flowering crocus, always plant in loose groups; in the bed, preferably between perennials that offer shade; also beautiful along the edges of shrubbery in front of a dark background and in the rock garden. **Zone:** 3–8.

EXPERT TIP
Pictured is the intensely colored variety 'Arendsii'.

GOOD PARTNERS
Low cushion perennials like thyme and grasses

Asters—Flowers Until Frost

Several Varieties of Early-flowering Asters

Species/Variety	Flower Color Of Special Note	Height (in/cm) When Flowers
Aster alpinus 'Albus' Alpine Aster	pure-white yellow center	8–12/20–30 May–June
Aster alpinus 'Dunkle Schöne' Alpine Aster	dark violet yellow center	12/30 May–June
Aster alpinus 'Happy End' Alpine Aster	pink various shades	10–12/25–30 May–June
Aster amellus 'Rudolph Goethe' Italian Aster	violet-blue	20/50 July–Sept
Aster amellus 'Lady Hindlip' Italian Aster	pink shaggy	24/60 July–Sept
Aster sedifolius 'Nanus' Wild dwarf Aster	blue yellow center	8–12/20–30 July–Aug
Aster sedifolius 'Nanus roseus' Wild dwarf Aster	pink yellow center	8–12/20–30 July–Aug
Aster tongolensis 'Berggarten' Early-summer Aster	lilac blue orange center	12–16/30–40 May–June
Aster tongolensis 'Berggartenzwerg' Early-summer Aster	brilliant blue orange center	8/20 May–June
Aster tongolensis 'Leuch- tenberg' Early-summer Aster	amethyst orange center	20/50 May–June

Several Varieties of Fall-flowering Asters

Species/Variety	Flower Color Of Special Note	Height (in/cm) When Flowers
Aster cordifolius Blue Wood Aster	lavender blue, lilac yellow-brown center	24–47/60–120 Sept–Nov
Aster divaricatus Fall Aster	white brown-yellow center	24–32/60–80 Sept–Oct
Aster dumosus hybrid 'Jenny' Michaelmas Daisy	violet purple yellow-brown center	12/30 Sept–Oct
Aster dumosus hybrid 'Nesthäkchen' Michaelmas Daisy	carmine pink yellow-brown center	10/25 Sept–Oct
Aster ericoides 'Erlkönig' Heath Aster	blue-violet yellowish center	47/120 Sept–Oct
Aster ericoides 'Ringdove' Heath Aster	pink yellow-brown center	35/90 Sept–Oct
Aster ericoides 'Schneegitter' Heath Aster	white yellow-brown center	39/100 Sept–Oct
Aster novae-angliae 'Barr's Blue' New England Aster	deep-blue yellow center	59/150 Sept
Aster novae-angliae 'Rubinschatz' New England Aster	ruby-red yellow center	47/120 Sept
Aster novi-belgii 'Dauerblau' Michaelmas Daisy	lilac blue yellow-brown center	59/150 Oct–Nov
Aster novi-belgii 'Fellowship' Michaelmas Daisy	pure pink, double yellow-brown center	35/90 Sept–Oct

Michaelmas Daisy, Aster

Aster novi-belgii, shown: 'Rubinkuppel'
Height/Width: 24–55 in (60–140 cm)/ 20–32 in (50–80 cm)
Blooms: September–October
Perennial

▶ **particularly large number of varieties**

Flowers: White, pink, crimson, light- to dark-blue, purple, violet, lilac, always with a yellow to brown eye, also semidouble and double (Ø up to $2^1/_2$ in [6 cm]). **Soil:** Fresh to moist, tolerates damp soils; nutrient-rich, humus, deeply cultivated, sandy or clayish soils improved with compost. **Care:** Provide organic-chemical fertil- izer in spring; water well during dry spells; stake high varieties; cut back after flowering. **Design:** Use as a showy perennial in the garden; put high varieties in the background. **Zone:** 4–9.

Michaelmas Daisy, Aster

Aster x *frikartii*, shown: 'Mönch'
Height/Width: 24–32 in (60–80 cm)/ 12–16 in (30–40 cm)
Blooms: August–September
Perennial

▶ **really superior hybrid**

Flowers: Blue to lilac, yellow center (Ø to $2^3/_4$ in [7 cm]). **Soil:** Dry to fresh; dry soils are well tolerated but not soggy ones or wet during winter; well-drained; nutrient-rich; alkaline. **Care:** Plant only in spring, since plants are very susceptible to damp- ness; fertilize sparingly and only with organic fertilizers, otherwise these hybrids are short-lived; cut back in fall. **Design:** Very suitable for sunny beds; plant far enough apart so that individual clusters of flowers show to best effect. **Zone:** 4/5–8. Likes winter protection in zone 5.

GOOD PARTNERS
Other fall-blooming asters, gayfeather, goldenrod

EXPERT TIP
Most common variety: 'Wonder of Staffa' (light violet-blue)

Of course asters are always considered the typical fall flower, but some species bloom earlier. Keep in mind when planning that some species grow very tall and may need staking.

New England Aster

Aster novae-angliae, shown: 'Rosa Sieger'
Height/Width: 39–63 in (100–160 cm)/
20–28 in (50–70 cm)
Blooms: September–October
Perennial

▶ **not rampant, mildew-proof**

Flowers: White, glowing pink, crimson, purple, violet to lavender-blue, dark-blue; they close less than the older varieties in dull weather and in evening (size varies widely according to variety, usually 1/2–11/2 in [2–4 cm]). **Soil:** Fresh, will also tolerate dryness for a short time; nutrient-rich, deeply cultivated; no heavy soils. **Care:** Fertilize with organic fertilizer in spring; water during dry spells; cut back after flowering. **Design:** Place in the back of the border as a focal point. **Zone:** 4–9.

Italian Aster

Aster amellus, shown: 'Violet Queen'
Height/Width: 16–24 in (40–60)/
12–16 in (30–40 cm)
Blooms: August–September
Wild perennial

▶ **has wildflower charm**

Flowers: Pink, violet blue, lilac, violet, with yellow center (Ø to 21/2 in [6 cm]). **Soil:** Moderately dry to fresh; dry soils are tolerated; no sogginess or winter wetness; well-drained; alkaline. **Care:** Plant only in spring, since the species is very water-sensitive; only fertilize sparingly or the plants will be short-lived and susceptible to disease; to prolong life in very rich soils, divide every 3 years. **Design:** Very beautiful in sunny perennial beds and in cottage gardens. **Zone:** 4–9.

Michaelmas Daisy, Aster

Aster dumosus hybrids
Height/Width: 6–8 in (15–20 cm)/
carpetlike
Blooms: August–October
Perennial

▶ **good ground cover in the bed**

Flowers: White, pink, carmine, red, blue, violet to lilac, center usually yellow (Ø 11/4–2 in [4–5 cm]). **Soil:** Fresh to moist, loamy, rich in humus, deeply cultivated. **Care:** Work in organic fertilizer in the spring; water plentifully during dry spells, which also prevents mildew; cut back after flowering; divide every 4 years, which keeps plants from getting bare and keeps them healthy. **Design:** Put tall varieties in the center and background of the beds; use low ones also as enclosures for beds; beautiful in the rock garden. **Zone:** 4–8.

GOOD PARTNERS
Other fall-flowering asters, heliopsis, gloriosa daisies

EXPERT TIP
Pictured is the variety 'Herbstgrüss'.

Grasses,

Ferns, and Ground Covers

The plants included in this group attract attention through their growth forms and foliage rather than the fullness and color of their flowers. Nevertheless, many of the ground covers also have attractive flowers.

In many gardens these plants are condemned to a truly shadowy existence. At most, the so-called ground covers are used for greening areas under trees and shrubs and there happily provide green but boring surfaces. This needn't be the case at all: Use combinations of ground covers that are appropriate to the particular location with varying heights, flower colors, and growth habits. Leave gaps between the ground covers where you can plant taller-growing perennials. And suddenly a monotonous carpet is transformed into a lively scene. Furthermore, you should select varieties that have colorful or textured foliage to gain color and leaf contrasts even after flowering is over.

Sunny Locations

The moss pink presented here is only one example of the many possibilities for decorating sunny areas with ground covers. Look in the garden centers among rock garden plants for other cushion perennials with widely spreading growth forms that can be used to design front gardens and pathways. Since many of these plants need sandy soil (ask when buying), you should prepare the place where they are to be planted appropriately. Used in the center of the bed, grasses, with their fan-shaped, spreading leaves, can also create a decorative contrast to perennials.

Shady, Damp Locations

In almost every garden there are some shady areas that often are damp as well. To the beginning gardener, it may seem simply impossible to beautifully design and plant such places. Here ferns and shade-tolerant grasses create wonderful and frequently very easy-care alternatives. Their various growth forms and foliage provide interest without flowers.

Much charm, even without flowers: a well planted shade garden.

Grasses— Austere Beauty

Quaking Grass
Briza media
Height/Width: 16–24 in (40–60 cm)/ 8–12 in (20–30 cm)
Blooms: May–June
Perennial

▶ **delicate, fluffy inflorescences**

Flowers: Flat, violet, heart-shaped spicules on gauzy, branching panicles. **Leaves:** Fresh green, narrow, forms light clumps. **Soil:** Any garden soil that is not too rich in nutrients; dry to fresh; well-drained. **Care:** Water during prolonged dry spells; fertilize very moderately. **Design:** Place in prairie-type and heath gardens in small, loose groups between large-leaved perennials; also suitable for rock gardens. **Zone:** 4/5–9.

Fescue
Festuca cinerea
Height/Width: 12–24 in (30–60 cm)/ 8–12 in (20–30 cm)
Blooms: June–July
Perennial

▶ **colorfully attractive grass**

Flowers: Compact flower panicles in the same color as the leaves; later golden. **Leaves:** Narrow, gray-green to steel-blue, depending on variety; stick out on all sides like a hedgehog; forms a hemispherical cushion. **Soil:** Moderately dry to dry, poor in humus and nutrients; sandy, well-drained; sogginess is not tolerated. **Care:** Remove dead material in spring; do not fertilize or the typical color will disappear and the grass will turn green. **Design:** Very beautiful by itself or in small groups in beds with lean soil or in the rock garden. **Zone:** 4–8.

Japanese Silver Grass
Miscanthus sinensis
Height/Width: 39–106 in [100–270 cm]/ 35–39 in [90–100 cm]
Blooms: September–October
Perennial

▶ **also very decorative in winter**

Flowers: Feathery panicles in creamy white, silver, brownish-red, or light-brown; decorative fruits. **Leaves:** Dark-green, linear with silvery center stripes on bamboolike blades, slightly pendulous; forms tall clumps. **Soil:** Fresh to moist; damp locations are also tolerated; rich in nutrients. **Care:** Cut back the leaves and fruit stalks in spring; fertilize at new growth; remove self-sown seedlings. **Design:** Beautiful as a specimen by the garden pond or in the background of a border. **Zone:** 5–9.

GOOD PARTNERS
Begonias, lady's mantle, campanulas

EXPERT TIP
Varieties: 'Kleine Fontäne' (pictured), 'Zebrinus', 'Gracillimus', 'Purpurascens', 'Yuku Jima'

Plant tall, striking grasses such as pampas grass as specimens between perennials. Smaller species usually work better in groups.

Fountain Grass
Pennisetum alopecuroides
Height/Width: 16–39 in (40–100 cm)/ up to 24 in (60 cm)
Blooms: September–October
Perennial

▶ **gracefully overhanging**

Flowers: Feathery, cattail-like blooms in light- to red-brown; variety 'Hameln' pictured. **Leaves:** Narrow, overhanging, gray-green, with golden-yellow fall coloring; forms broad clumps. **Soil:** Moderately dry to moist; does not tolerate very dry, sandy, or any compacted soils. **Care:** In spring cut back; fertilize occasionally; water during long dry spells. **Design:** As a specimen plant or in small groups in the bed; also on a slope. **Zone:** 6/7–9.

Japanese Sedge Grass
Carex morrowii 'Variegata'
Height/Width: 16–20 in (40–50 cm)/12–16 in (30–40 cm)
Blooms: Not significant
Perennial

▶ **winter-green to evergreen**

Flowers: Insignificant, yellow flowers in clusters of ears. **Leaves:** Broad, arching, dark-green with yellow stripes at the sides; forms shallow clumps. **Soil:** Any humusy garden soil; fresh to moist; tolerates neither dryness nor sogginess. **Care:** Remove spotty leaves in spring; water during dry spells. **Design:** Thrives and looks nice between open woody plants or in the shade of hedges and walls; plant singly or in groups. **Zone:** 5/6–9.

Pampas Grass
Cortaderia selloana
Height/Width: 47–102 in (120–260 cm)/ 59–71 in (150–180 cm)
Blooms: September–October
Perennial

▶ **very dominating plant**

Flowers: Large, silky, silvery-white panicles (20–28 in [50–70 cm] tall). **Leaves:** Narrow, long with sharp edges; gray-green; forms tall clumps. **Soil:** Fresh, also dry for short periods; deeply cultivated; well-drained; rich in nutrients. **Care:** Cut back previous year's leaves in the spring; fertilize heavily; water during long dry spells; in late fall tie up the leaves into a shock as winter protection and pack with dry leaves. **Design:** Must only be used as a specimen; beautiful at the edge of a lawn and in front of walls; also in pebble beds. **Zone:** 8–11.

GOOD PARTNERS
Asters, fall chrysanthemums, lady's mantle

EXPERT TIP
Related: Sedge grass (C. pendula), up to 59 in (150 cm) tall

EXPERT TIP
Varieties: 'Sunningdale Silver' (79 in [200 cm]), 'Pumila' (up to 59 in [150 cm])

Ferns—from Filigreed to Robust

Northern Maidenhair Fern
Adiantium pedatum
Height/Width: 16–24 in (40–60 cm)/
up to 39 in (100 cm)
Blooms: no flowers, forms spores
Perennial

▶ **striking fans of leaves**

Leaves: Bright-green fronds of delicate, wavy leaflets, arranged in fans; forms broad clumps; fall color golden yellow. **Soil:** Damp to fresh; damp soils are tolerated; well-drained; rich in humus. **Care:** In spring mulch heavily with leaf compost or pine needles; cover at any threat of late frost; weed out aggressive neighbors; leave undisturbed. **Design:** Ideal in a noticeable spot under light shrubs; also in semishady beds or rock gardens. **Zone:** 3–8. Does not thrive in climates warmer than zone 8.

Soft Shield Fern
Polystichum setiferum
Height/Width: 20–39 in (50–100 cm)/
24–47 in (60–120 cm)
Blooms: no flowers, develops spores
Perennial

▶ **loose funnel-shaped clumps**

Leaves: Dull green, bipinnate, lacy, soft, almost like terrycloth; fronds narrow-lanceolate, loose and elegantly overhanging, forms funnel-shaped clumps or loose bunches; stays green in winter in mild climates. **Soil:** Fresh to moist, loose, rich in humus. **Care:** Mulch in fall with leaf humus; water and sprinkle with water in spring and summer during longer dry spells. **Design:** Especially beautiful under light shrubbery; in deeply dug, damp soils, also on the north side of walls. **Zone:** 3–8. Does not thrive in climates warmer than zone 8.

Hart's Tongue Fern
Phyllitis scolopendrium
Height/Width: 8–16 in (20–40 cm)/
8–12 in (20–30 cm)
Blooms: no flowers, develops spores
Winter-green perennial

▶ **unusual leaf form**

Leaves: Bright green, shining, tongue-shaped, undivided, leathery, edges slightly wavy, forms broad clumps. **Soil:** Fresh to moist; well-drained; rich in humus, even slightly acid; tolerates wet soils; do not put in slightly dry situations. **Care:** Mix in leaf compost when planting; remove previous year's leaves when new growth first appears; protect from late frosts; in fall mulch with leaf compost. **Design:** Ideal for shady, wind-protected areas of the garden; because of its small size, belongs in the foreground. **Zone:** 3–8.

EXPERT TIP
There are many varieties, including dwarf forms as well.

EXPERT TIP
One of the most beautiful ferns, with many varieties

GOOD PARTNERS
Lacy ferns, Solomon's seal (polygonatum), sweet woodruff

Add variety to shady areas with many ferns of graduated sizes and growth forms combined with wildflowers.

Male Fern

Dryopteris filix-mas
Height/Width: 20–43 in (50–110 cm)/ 32–39 in (80–100 cm)
Blooms: no flowers, forms spores
Perennial

▶ robust native fern

Leaves: Upper side dull green, underside lighter, bipinnate, fronds slightly overhanging, forms funnel-shaped clumps. **Soil:** Fresh to moist, loose; one of the few ferns that also tolerates short periods of dryness. **Care:** Mulch occasionally with leaf mulch; water during protracted dry spells. **Design:** Suitable for woodland gardens, semishady to shady areas of the garden such as along wooded areas; also for sunny places if there is enough moisture in the soil.
Zone: 3/4–9.

Ostrich Fern

Matteuccia pensylvanica
Height/Width: 24–55 in (60–140 cm)/ up to 39 in (100 cm)
Blooms: no flowers, forms spores
Perennial

▶ beautiful form, develops runners, native fern

Leaves: Fresh green, bipinnate; the ostrich feather-like fronds are arranged in a vase shape. **Soil:** Fresh to moist; occasional wetness is tolerated but not constantly; loose; rich in humus. **Care:** Water plentifully during dry spells; mulch with leaf humus in fall; if growth is too vigorous, cut back the runners.
Design: Best planted in light shade of woodsy shrubs or in front of a hedge; only use one or a few plants, since the species needs a lot of space because it forms runners. **Zone:** 3/4–8.

Royal Fern

Osmunda regalis
Height/Width: 24–79 in (60–200 cm)/ 47–59 in (120–150 cm)
Blooms: no flowers, develops spores
Perennial

▶ largest native fern

Leaves: Fresh green, bipinnate, yellow in fall. **Soil:** Moist to wet, loose, rich in humus, acid. **Care:** When planting—preferably in spring—mix in peat; mulch regularly with leaf humus or pine needles; water lavishly, especially when ferns receive much sunlight. **Design:** Beautiful planted under light shrubbery or in the background of shade beds, in sufficiently damp soil even in sunny areas of the garden; do not dig out any wild plants.
Zone: 3–9.

GOOD PARTNERS
Hosta, campanulas, rhododendron

GOOD PARTNERS
Japanese sedge and other grasses, hostas, goatsbeard

Ground Covers— Flowering Carpets

Carpet Bugleweed
Ajuga reptans
Height/Width: 6–8 in (15–20 cm)/
up to 20 in (50 cm)
Blooms: April–May
Perennial

▶ **undemanding, vigorous**

Flowers: Depending on variety, white, pink, purplish pink, blue, brilliant blue (Ø $1/4$ in [5–8 mm]) on thick, candle-like inflorescences. **Soil:** Fresh to moist, also will tolerate wet soils; nutrient-rich; loamy. **Care:** Fertilize with organic fertilizer in spring; water during dry spells; the species spreads by means of runners, which can be kept under control by chopping back. **Design:** Suitable for the edge of a wooded area, in front of loose hedges and on stream banks; there are also varieties with decorative brownish-red or white variegated leaves. **Zone:** 3–8. Does not thrive in warmer climates.

Pachysandra
Pachysandra terminalis
Height/Width: 8–12 in (20–30 cm)/
24 in (60 cm)
Blooms: April–May
Subshrub

▶ **evergreen, problem-free**

Flowers: White, small, in short, roll-shaped spikes; not very noticeable. **Soil:** Fresh, loose, humusy, slightly acid. **Care:** In spring, fertilize sparingly with organic fertilizer; water during extended dry spells; plants that are growing well need scarcely any care. **Design:** Ideal as an undemanding substitute for grass and under high and low shrubs; is usually planted shallowly; there is also a variety with decorative, white-bordered leaves. **Zone:** 3–8.

Myrtle, Common Periwinkle
Vinca minor
Height/Width: 4–8 in (10–20 cm)/
up to 47 in (120 cm)
Blooms: April–May
Subshrub

▶ **evergreen and vigorous**

Flowers: Light-blue, also brilliant blue, white, and red, also doubled (Ø $1/4$ in [1 cm]). **Soil:** Moderately dry to moist; also tolerates cool, damp spots; loose; humusy. **Care:** Fertilize with a layer of rich compost in fall; the long shoots form roots at leaf nodes on surface; if necessary, cut the plants back to the desired size. **Design:** Outstanding ground cover under shrubs and in the shade of walls; only put with very vigorous plants, since the myrtle will overwhelm anything less vigorous. **Zone:** 3–9.

GOOD PARTNERS
*Epimedium, large ferns,
lady's mantle*

EXPERT TIP
*The variety 'Variegata' has
white-variegated leaves.*

Don't plant large areas monotonously with one ground cover. It's better to combine several species with differing leaves and flowers.

Spotted Dead Nettle
Lamium maculatum
Height/Width: 6–16 in (15–40 cm)/
24 in (60 cm)
Blooms: May–June
Wild perennial

▶ **many interesting varieties**

Flowers: Lilac purple, in whorls, also white, pinkish purple, and violet rose (Ø up to ¼ in [1 cm]). **Soil:** Fresh to moist; wet soils are tolerated; loose; nutrient-rich. **Care:** Mulch with humus in fall or spring; cut back any shoots that are too vigorous; water only during prolonged dry spells. **Design:** Very beautiful planted in carpets under shrubbery or in the shadow of walls and hedges; there are varieties with silvery spots or striped leaves, which lighten the look of dim areas. **Zone:** 3–8.

Creeping Forget-Me-Not
Omphalodes verna
Height/Width: 4–8 in (10–20 cm)/
12–24 in (30–60)
Blooms: March–May
Perennial

▶ **gives a very natural effect**

Flowers: Brilliant blue with white center, also pure-white varieties (Ø about ¼ in [1 cm]). **Soil:** Fresh to moist; also wet soils are tolerated; loose; humusy; alkaline. **Care:** Occasionally fertilize in spring with a layer of compost; only water during prolonged dry spells. The species spreads through runners and must be cut back to the desired size if necessary. **Design:** Beautiful under and in front of shrubs, in front of walls, in the shaded edge areas of borders. **Zone:** 5–8.

Moss Pink
Phlox subulata hybrids
Height/Width: 2–6 in (5–15 cm)/
up to 24 in (60 cm)
Blooms: April–May
Cushion perennial

▶ **heavy bloomer in full sun**

Flowers: Depending on variety, pure-white, salmon pink, glowing pink, purple-red, carmine, slate-blue, or violet (Ø 2–2½ in [5–6 cm]). **Soil:** Moderately dry to fresh, also tolerates dry soils; well-drained; nutrient-rich. **Care:** Water only sparingly and fertilize moderately; after blooming cut the cushion back to half height; this will keep it compact and promote flowering again in the fall. **Design:** Beautiful as a ground cover in the rock garden, as a bed enclosure, on tops of walls, and on sunny slopes. **Zone:** 4–9.

GOOD PARTNERS
Grasses, pulmonaria,
Solomon's seal

EXPERT TIP
Related: Navelwort
(O. cappadocica)

GOOD PARTNERS
Aubrieta, delicate grasses,
baby's-breath

Trees and Shrubs

These plants form stable, woody shoots and roots and can grow much taller than perennials and summer flowers. Their permanence makes them the supporting framework of any garden design.

Proceed with caution when planting trees and shrubs in the garden. Bear in mind that the woody plants are very long-lived and often grow very slowly. They usually look so tiny immediately after you buy them that it is easy to lose sight of how large they are going to be eventually. Even if it seems ever so enticing, don't buy and plant too many woody plants! For the first few years it's better to fill in the gaps with perennials. They can more easily be removed later than shrubs and trees that are planted too close together.

The Right Tree

First choose the large woody plants. For most smaller yards a single tree as a focal point or next to the house is enough. This can be a purely ornamental tree, but it definitely can also be a fruit tree. These may need a pollinating partner, which you can check by asking or looking it up. In this case you should choose a variety that partners a tree already present in the neighborhood or plant a pair in cooperation with a neighbor.

Choosing Shrubs

In very small yards, a large shrub can be an appropriate substitute for a tree. But it can also require even more space, so its location demands just as careful planning. Medium-sized shrubs usually create the background for beds or are planted as a screen for the terrace.

Smaller shrubs are almost universally appropriate. They can be used for hedges or enclosures or create accents in perennial beds. But always choose the shrub's colors of leaves (fall color, too) and flowers to go with the perennials in its vicinity.

Trees and shrubs shape the garden picture throughout the entire year.

Trees—the Backbone of the Large Yard

Japanese Flowering Cherry
Prunus serrulata
Height/Width: 13–33 ft (4–10 m)/
13–26 ft (4–8 m)
Blooms: April–June
Shrub or tree

▶ **flowers lavishly**

Flowers: Depending on variety, white, light- to dark-pink, single, semi-double to double, slightly fragrant (Ø up to 2$^1/_2$ in [6 cm]). **Soil:** Well-drained; dry soils are also tolerated; humus-rich; alkaline. **Care:** Remove suckers that grow out of the bud union; no pruning necessary. **Design:** Very well suited to use as a specimen; as necessary, choose from the many varieties that grow to various heights and breadths to columnar shape; also form weeping crowns. **Zone:** 5–9.

Crab Apple
Malus hybrids
Height/Width: up to 26 ft (8 m)/
up to 33 ft (10 m)
Blooms: April–May
Tree or large shrub

▶ **spreading growth habit**

Flowers: Pink, red, ruby-, lilac- to dark-red (Ø 1–2 in [3–5 cm]). **Leaves:** With some varieties new growth is brownish-red, later glossy green; fall coloring, depending on variety, yellow, orange, red, brownish-red. **Soil:** Deeply cultivated, humus-rich, not too dry and sandy; neutral to acid. **Care:** Mulch around the bottom to the drip-line; occasionally thin old trees. **Design:** Effective either as a specimen plant or also very good in loose groups. **Zone:** 4–8.

Black Locust, False Acacia
Robinia pseudoacacia 'Umbraculifera'
Height/Width: 13–20 ft (4–6 m)/
13 ft (4 m)
Blooms: none
Globe-shaped tree

▶ **very decorative crown**

Flowers: This variety does not bloom; white, fragrant flowers appear in June only on the 66-ft (20-m) tall wild variety. **Leaves:** Pinnate, on thorny branches; yellow in fall. **Soil:** Dry to fresh; alkaline; damp and acid situations unsuitable. **Care:** The variety develops a globular crown without any pruning; but it can also be very severely pruned into shape. **Design:** It looks quite stunning as a clearly visible specimen in the lawn; its roots inhibit the growth of other woody plants! **Zone:** 3–9.

EXPERT TIP
Double varieties: 'Hokusai' (light-pink), 'Kanzan' (dark-pink). Ask for disease resistant varieties.

EXPERT TIP
Other varieties: 'Frisia' (looser crown, golden-yellow leaves)

Choose trees with thought! Especially in the small yard, one well-placed tree creates a better effect than a group of trees, which also cast much more shade.

Weeping Birch
Betula pendula 'Youngii'
Height/Width: 16–23 ft (5–7 m)/ 13 ft (4 m)
Blooms: March–April
Tree

▶ **dainty and decorative**

Flowers: Yellow hanging catkins. **Leaves:** Fresh-green, yellow in fall. **Soil:** Dry to fresh, well-drained, nutrient-rich. **Care:** No special pruning and maintenance measures except watering during prolonged dry spells. **Design:** The weeping birch works best as a specimen and as a backdrop for a perennial bed or a sitting area; it's essential when buying to ask for the lower-growing, garden form, for the wild weeping birch grows to over 66 ft (20 m); the variety 'Gracilis', to use another example, is only 10–16 ft (3–5 m) tall. **Zone:** 2–7.

European Mountain Ash, Rowan
Sorbus acuparia
Height/Width: 16–49 ft (5–15 m)/ depends on variety
Blooms: May
Tree or shrub

▶ **several fruiting and ornamental varieties**

Flowers: White corymbs, strong spicy odor, from which develop coral-red berries; there are especially large-fruited varieties that are planted as wild fruit. **Leaves:** Pinnate; orange-red fall coloring. **Soil:** Nutrient-rich, deeply cultivated, moderately dry. **Care:** Fertilize with compost in spring; no pruning necessary. **Design:** The low-growing, columnar ornamental forms and the standards are particularly good as specimens; the shrublike forms are effective in groups and hedges. **Zone:** 3–7. Does not do well in warmer climates.

Japanese Maple
Acer palmatum 'Atropurpureum'
Height/Width: 13–20 ft (4–6 m)/ 7–16 ft (2–5 m)
Blooms: May–June
Tree or shrub

▶ **optimal for small gardens**

Flowers: Purplish-red in clusters, from which reddish, winged little nuts develop. **Leaves:** Depending on species, yellow, green to dark-red, and with varying spectacular fall coloring. **Soils:** Well-drained, slightly acid, slightly moist. **Care:** Water thoroughly during dry spells; otherwise leave undisturbed. **Design:** The varieties work best as specimens; take time when making your choice; there are around 200 (!) varieties altogether with differing heights, growth habits, and colors. **Zone:** 5–8.

EXPERT TIP
Varieties: 'Fastigiata' (columnar), 'Pendula' (weeping)

GOOD PARTNERS
Underplanting with forget-me-nots or false miterwort

Small Trees and Large Shrubs

Chinese Magnolia, Saucer Magnolia
Magnolia x soulangiana
Height/Width: up to 20 ft (6 m)/ up to 13 ft (4 m)
Blooms: April–May
Shrub

▶ **incomparable spring flowers**

Flowers: Appear before the leaves; depending on variety or hybrid, white to pink, also bicolored and striped; intensely fragrant (Ø to 4 in [10 cm]). **Leaves:** Large, oval, green. **Soil:** Slightly acid to neutral, moist, well-drained, nutrient-rich, neither dry nor compacted. **Care:** Mulch the root area in fall as a protection against freezing; do not injure the roots with digging; do not cut shoots; the flowers are damaged by late frosts, but not the tree. **Design:** Unparalleled as a specimen; also in a small front yard. **Zone:** 4–9.

Smokebush
Cotinus coggygria
Height/Width: up to 16 ft (5 m)/ up to 13 ft (4 m)
Blooms: June–July
Shrub

▶ **delicate, light inflorescences**

Flowers: Whitish flowers in large panicles, remaining on bush a long time; from these the wiglike red fruit clusters develop, beginning in July. **Leaves:** Lanceolate-oval, depending on variety green or dark red with orange to red fall coloring. **Soil:** Dry to fresh, alkaline, sandy-loamy. **Care:** Do not prune, to maintain the fullness of bloom and allow the natural growth form to develop. **Design:** Beautiful in a specimen planting or as a focus point in a loose shrubbery grouping. **Zone:** 4–8.

Serviceberry, Shadbush
Amelanchier lamarckii
Height/Width: 16–26 ft (5–8 m)/ 10–16 ft (3–5 m)
Blooms: April–May
Shrub or tree

▶ **undemanding and decorative**

Flowers: Appear before the foliage; creamy-white in long racemes, smelling like honey, from which the small, purplish red fruits develop in August; these are edible raw. **Leaves:** Oval, dark-green, yellow to orange-red fall color. **Soil:** Any normal garden soil, alkaline, also dry. **Care:** This undemanding species needs no special pruning or maintenance. **Design:** Beautiful alone or with several as a loose flowering hedge, as a specimen in the background of the garden or as a backdrop for bulb plantings. **Zone:** 4–9.

EXPERT TIP
Related: Star magnolia (M. stellata, white)

GOOD PARTNERS
Beautiful in front of a backdrop of dark conifers

EXPERT TIP
Relative: Weeping serviceberry (A. laevis); A. arborea is an excellent choice

Small trees and large shrubs are especially versatile: You can use them as specimen accents where space is limited and give structure to hedges and groups of woody plants.

Common Lilac

Syringa vulgaris hybrids
Height/Width: up to 20 ft (6 m)/ up to 16 ft (5 m)
Blooms: May
Shrub

▶ **classic flowering shrub**

Flowers: Depending on variety, white, yellow, pink, purple, lilac-red ('Charles Joly', pictured above), also bicolored, single or doubled, in upright, roller-shaped panicles. **Leaves:** Broad oval, sturdy green. **Soil:** Well-drained, nutrient-rich, alkaline, also in dry soils. **Care:** Give potassium fertilizer when new growth appears; remove suckers at the base; cut off spent flowers. **Design:** Very beautiful alone as a focal point the back of the border, also in hedges and groups of shrubs. **Zone:** 3–7.

European Euonymus Tree

Euonymus europaea
Height/Width: up to 20 ft (6 m)/ up to 13 ft (4 m)
Blooms: May
Shrub or small tree

▶ **attractive, poisonous fruits**

Flowers: Unobtrusive yellow green, in one variety rose-red; from the flowers develop poisonous, four-lobed crimson fruits in August. **Leaves:** Elliptical, light-green, yellow to carmine-red in fall. **Soil:** Dry to fresh, alkaline, nutrient-rich. **Care:** Mulch with compost before new growth appears, which leads to a more abundant fruit production; do not prune so that the typical growth form can develop. **Design:** Decorative as a specimen, also in shrubbery groups, screens, and hedges. **Zone:** 3–7.

Staghorn Sumac

Rhus typhina
Height/Width: up to 13 ft (4 m)/ up to 20 ft (6 m)
Blooms: June–July
Treelike shrub

▶ **splendid fall foliage**

Flowers: Green in candlelike panicles, from which coblike, reddish-brown, poisonous fruit clusters develop starting in August. **Leaves:** Large, pinnate, poisonous, in fall orange-scarlet. **Soil:** Normal, dry to moist garden soil. **Care:** Leave the root region undisturbed and do not injure the roots with digging, since otherwise suckers develop; every year persistently remove any suckers that come up. **Design:** As a specimen it needs sufficient space; can also be planted in a loose shrub group. **Zone:** 3–8.

GOOD PARTNERS
Shadbush, hazelnut,
black elder

EXPERT TIP
Varieties: '*Dissecta*' *(leaves fernlike),*
'*Laciniata*' *(leaves laciniated)*

Versatile Small Shrubs

Japanese Rose
Kerria japonica 'Pleniflora'
Height/Width: up to 7 ft (2 m)/ up to 5 ft (1.5 m)
Blooms: May
Shrub

▶ **lush bloom, undemanding**

Flowers: Golden-yellow, double, buttercuplike and round (Ø about 2 in [5 cm]). **Leaves:** Lanceolate-oval, fresh-green, form a beautiful contrast to the flowers. **Soil:** The plant thrives happily in any garden soil. **Care:** Little fertilizing or scarcely any flowers will develop, but many suckers; after a severe winter take out frozen branches; regularly cut back old ones and remove superfluous suckers. **Design:** Ideal as an element in a hedge or in loose groups; has little personality as a single specimen. **Zone:** 4–9.

Firethorn
Pyracantha coccinea
Height/Width: 7–10 ft (2–3 m)/ up to 7 ft (2 m)
Blooms: May–June
Evergreen shrub

▶ **fiery fall ornament**

Flowers: White, rather insignificant, from which develop, beginning in August, small fruits, that are yellow, orange, or red, depending on the variety. **Leaves:** Small, glossy, dark-green, on thorny branches; in exposed situations merely winter-green. **Soil:** Undemanding; thrives in any—even dry—garden soil. **Care:** Needs no pruning but can be staked into shape; remove winter-killed branches in spring. **Design:** Beautiful in front of a house wall or in hedges. **Zone:** 5–9.

Forsythia
Forsythia x *intermedia*
Height/Width: 3–13 ft (1–4 m)/ up to 8 ft (2.5 m)
Blooms: April
Shrub

▶ **glorious and early-flowering**

Flowers: Countless yellow flowers, which appear before the foliage; many varieties from light- to egg-yolk yellow. **Leaves:** Matte green, small leaflets. **Soil:** Any normal garden soil; fresh; nutrient-rich. **Care:** Regular organic fertilizing; every 3–4 years remove old branches so that the shrub will keep on blooming heavily. **Design:** Ideal in a shrub group or hedge, where it is very visible in bloom in the spring; low-growing varieties also suitable for the rock garden or containers. **Zone:** 4–9.

EXPERT TIP
'Kasan' and 'Lalandei' are best in colder (zone 5) areas.

GOOD PARTNERS
Botanical tulips, grape hyacinths, blue squill

Small shrubs are most effective in beds or in loose groups. Play with different heights, growth forms, and color.

Rhododendron
Rododendron hybrids
Height/Width: up to 13 ft (4 m)/
up to 13 ft (4 m)
Blooms: April–June
Evergreen shrub

▶ **many hybrids and varieties**

Flowers: Depending on subspecies, white, yellow, orange, pink, red, violet, in dense clusters; also streaked with other colors. **Leaves:** Leathery, glossy. **Soil:** Rich in humus, well-drained, acid. **Care:** Acidify the soil if necessary when planting by adding peat or pine needles or use special rhododendron fertilizer from the nursery; mulch root region; do not injure roots; twist off faded flowers; water thoroughly during dry spells. **Design:** As groups in woodsy shade; coordinate their flowering times. **Zone:** 4–8.

Weigelia
Weigelia hybrids
Height/Width: up to 10 ft (3 m)/
up to 10 ft (3 m)
Blooms: May–July
Shrub

▶ **heavy bloomer, many varieties**

Flowers: Depending on variety, light-pink to dark-red; bell-shaped on arching, overhanging branches. **Leaves:** Oval, fresh-green, form a beautiful contrast to the flowers. **Soil:** Normal, well-maintained garden soil, nutrient-rich. **Care:** In spring fertilize with organic fertilizer and mulch with compost; regularly cut out the oldest branches at the base so that the fullness of flowering is maintained. **Design:** Very beautiful as a single focal point in the background of the bed or as a hedge shrub. **Zone:** 5–8.

Double File Viburnum
Viburnum plicatum var. *tomentosum*
Height/Width: up to 7 ft (2 m)/
up to 10 ft (3 m)
Blooms: May–June
Shrub

▶ **effect is very exotic**

Flowers: White in $2^1/_2$–3 in (6–8 cm) wide broad, flat panicles, from which, rarely, blue-black, poisonous berries are formed in September. **Leaves:** Lanceolate, dark-green; in fall, wine-red to violet. **Soil:** Any fresh, humusy, well-drained garden soil. **Care:** Apply organic fertilizer occasionally; now and then remove branches that are too close together to create a loose growth form. **Design:** A single specimen is effective as are loose groups and hedges. **Zone:** 5–8.

EXPERT TIP
Azaleas are deciduous rhododendrons.

EXPERT TIP
Pictured is the large-flowered variety 'Mariesii'.

Evergreen Woody Plants

English Holly
Ilex aquifolium
Height/Width: 7–16 ft (2–5 m)/ 13 ft (4 m)
Blooms: May
Broad-leaved evergreen

▶ **good defensive hedge plant**

Flowers: White, insignificant, from which in September female plants develop poisonous fruits, red or yellow, depending on variety (Ø $1/2$ in [7–10 mm]). **Leaves:** Medium- to dark-green, depending on variety, also white to yellow bordered or marbled gray-green, glossy, leathery, spiny. **Soil:** Fresh, loose, rich in humus. **Care:** Water plentifully in fall; mulch root area; if necessary, protect by shading from drying winter sun; in spring fertilize with organic fertilizer. **Design:** Beautiful in shrub groups and unclipped hedges. **Zone:** 6–9.

White Spruce
Picea glauca
Height/Width: up to 50 ft (15 m)/ up to 8 ft (2.5 m)
Blooms: April–May
Conifer

▶ **dwarf and cone-shaped forms**

Flowers: Insignificant, from which in October develop brown, unobtrusive cones. **Needles:** Depending on variety, light-gray to blue-green, stiff and sharp. **Soil:** Well-drained, fresh to somewhat damp, slightly acid to alkaline. **Care:** Water during prolonged dry spells; disturbing branches can be removed. **Design:** The variety is very suitable for use as a hedge, windscreen, and the cone specimen in the border, spreading dwarf forms for rock gardens, and also planters. **Zone:** 2–6.

Common Juniper
Juniperus communis
Height/Width: 5–10 ft (1.5–3 m)/ 8–12 ft (2.5–3.5 m)
Blooms: April–May
Conifer

▶ **important for gardens with sandy and drier soils**

Flowers: Insignificant, from which in September develop blue-black berry cones, the juniper berries. **Needles:** Depending on variety, blue-gray to -green, sharp, but not prickly. **Soil:** All soils, also dry and poor. **Care:** Tie older columnar forms together if they threaten to fall apart. **Design:** Columnar varieties give height to a heather garden; or the dwarf forms can be used in the rock garden and planters; creeping varieties are also good ground covers. **Zone:** 2–7.

EXPERT TIP
Pictured is the variety 'Argenteo marginata'.

EXPERT TIP
Pictured is the variety 'Echiniformis'.

EXPERT TIP
'Compressa' and 'Depressa' are good dwarf forms.

As specimens, evergreens provide a focal point throughout the entire year. But too many of them quickly make the garden appear very dark.

American Arborvitae
Thuja occidentalis
Height/Width: 40–60 ft (12–18 m)/ 10–15 ft (3–5 m)
Blooms: March–May
Conifer

▶ **great variety of forms**

Flowers: Insignificant, from which, beginning in September, develop poisonous, greenish to brown, oval to lanceolate cones. **Needles:** Scale-formed, aromatically fragrant, poisonous, depending on variety yellow, bronze, fresh-, dark-, or blue-green, often browning in winter. **Soil:** All garden soils so long as they contain sufficient moisture. **Care:** Fertilize occasionally. **Design:** Columnar shapes are good specimens; dwarf forms are beautiful in rock gardens; some varieties are also suitable for clipped hedges. **Zone:** 2–8.

Mugo Pine
Pinus mugo
Height/Width: 15–20 ft (4.5–6 m)/ 25–30 ft (8–9 m)
Blooms: April–May
Conifer

▶ **many forms and varieties**

Flowers: Male flowers spikelike, female insignificant, from which even in young plants form oval, brown cones starting in July. **Needles:** Dark-green to gray-blue, stiff, occurring in pairs. **Soil:** Well-drained, humusy, moderately dry to moist, also lean. **Care:** If possible, do not prune so that the shrub can develop typically. **Design:** The dwarf forms go well in heather or rock gardens or planters; taller-growing ones should be used as specimen plants or in groups. **Zone:** 2–7.

Sawara Cypress
Chamaecyparis pisifera
Height/Width: up to 16 ft (5 m)/ up to 13 ft (4 m)
Blooms: March–May
Conifer

▶ **robust and versatile**

Flowers: Insignificant, from which, starting in October, develop small, brown, conical cones. **Needles:** scale-shaped, depending on variety golden-yellow, bronze, fresh-green to silver-gray-blue. **Soil:** Any garden soil that is well-drained and not too dry. **Care:** If necessary, protect yellow-needled forms in winter from strong sun and drying winds with burlap. **Design:** Dwarf forms for rock gardens or slopes; taller varieties with feathering branches ('Filifera . . .') as accent plants in the front or back yard. **Zone:** 3–8.

EXPERT TIP
Varieties 'Columna' (column), 'Danica' (spherical), 'Holmstrup' (cone)

EXPERT TIP
Flattened conical, low varieties: 'Compressa' and 'Filifera nana'

Fruit Trees—Productive and Beautiful

Black Currant
Ribes nigrum
Height/Width: 3–6 ft (1–1.8 m)/ about 5 ft (1.5 m)
Blooms: April
Shrub

▶ **especially large amount of vitamin C**

Flowers: Greenish-yellow clusters. **Fruits:** Black; depending on variety, medium- to large-sized, with intensely colored juice. **Soil:** Moderately heavy, humusy, nutrient-rich. **Harvest and Care:** Fruits ripen for picking June–August; water during protracted dry spells; mulch the root region regularly; cut out the exhausted old canes every year in winter; they are recognizable by their dark color. **Design:** Beautiful as an element in a hedge or enclosing a cottage garden. **Zone:** 2–7.

Sweet Cherry
Prunus avium
Height/Width: 16–33 ft (5–10 m)/ 13–30 ft (4–9 m)
Blooms: April–May
Tree

▶ **also less rampantly growing forms**

Flowers: White to pink; second pollinating variety necessary. **Fruit:** Large, depending on variety, violet, red, orange, or yellow. **Soil:** Nutrient-rich, loose, deeply cultivated. **Harvest and Care:** Fruits ready to harvest from May–July, depending on variety; mulch tree to dripline with compost; in severe climates, paint with protective trunk paint against frost; training pruning during first few years recommended. **Design:** Best for larger yards, since sweet cherries need an area of up to 861 ft² (80 m²), depending on variety and grafting stock. **Zone:** 3.

Sour Cherry
Prunus cerasus
Height/Width: 7–23 ft (2–7 m)/ 7–13 ft (2–4 m)
Blooms: April–May
Tree

▶ **one tree per family is enough**

Flowers: White; most varieties do not need an additional pollinating variety. **Fruits:** Depending on variety, small to large; light- to dark-red, brown-violet. **Soil:** Well aerated, also less fruitful soils. **Harvest and Care:** Fruits are ready to harvest, depending on variety, July–August. Thin out branches after harvest; about every 10 years carry out rejuvenation pruning, or the tree grows bare otherwise. **Design:** Beautiful as a specimen in a meadow as a focal point or as an element in a loose group of woody plants. **Zone:** 4–8.

EXPERT TIP
Better to plant two varieties as pollinators

GOOD PARTNERS
Several pollinators should grow in the vicinity.

EXPERT TIP
Varieties: 'Montmorency', 'Evans', and 'English Morello'

Many kinds have splendid spring flowers, some also have a pretty growth form, but all have the additional advantage of bearing delicious fruit.

European Elderberry
Sambucus nigra
Height/Width: 13–23 ft (4–7 m)/ 13–16 ft (4–5 m)
Blooms: May–June
Shrub

▶ **undemanding hedge shrub**

Flowers: Creamy-white, fragrant, in wide umbel-like panicles; are also enjoyed in thin pastry deep-fried in oil. **Fruits:** Small, black fruits in hanging panicles, edible cooked. **Soil:** Fresh to moist, nutrient-rich. **Harvest and Care:** Fruits ready to harvest August–September; mulch root region regularly and fertilize organically; tolerates heavy cutting back. **Design:** Pretty in a loose hedge and also beside the compost heap. **Zone:** 3–9.

Common Apple
Malus spp.
Height/Width: 6–33 ft (2–10 m)/ 8–40 ft (2–12 m)
Blooms: May
Tree

▶ **also less spreading forms**

Flowers: White to pink-hued, needs a pollinator in the vicinity. **Fruits:** Depending on variety medium to large, green, yellow, orange, or red. **Soil:** Any maintained garden soil, somewhat protected location. **Harvest and Care:** Depending on variety, picking from August to October; regular pruning recommended; keep the area under the tree clear and mulch. **Design:** As specimens, small forms with globular crowns are beautiful; slower-growing forms can also be espaliered against a sunny wall. **Zone:** 3–9.

Plum
Prunus domestica
Height/Width: 12–20 ft (3–6 m)/ 10–20 (3–6 m)
Blooms: April–May
Tree

▶ **many forms and varieties**

Flowers: White; some varieties need a pollinator variety nearby. **Fruit:** Plums roundish, yellow, red, or purple, damsons oval to egg-shaped, with a seam, blue to violet. **Soil:** Fresh, nutrient-rich, well-drained, wind-protected location. **Harvest and Care:** Depending on variety, ready for picking July–September; mulch under the tree; in severe climates protect the trunk with painting against frost cracks; prune the crown regularly; fertilize in spring. **Design:** Most beautiful in a small fruit garden. **Zone:** 4–9.

EXPERT TIP
'Johns' and 'Adams 2' are recommended cultivars.

EXPERT TIP
Other forms: 'Damson', 'Mount Royal', and 'Santa Rosa'

Roses

Opinion is divided on roses: Some love them for their beautiful flowers and their fragrance, others avoid them because of their requirements for somewhat more time-consuming care.

Indeed, roses are among the fussier plants. They need deeply cultivated soil, plenty of water, pruning, many hours of sun daily, and often are susceptible to diseases and pests. Therefore beginners should approach roses with respect. Preferably you should first plant an especially robust variety in the perennial bed. Water, fertilize, and prune your rose as required, and evaluate your progress.

Practice Makes Perfect

If you are successful growing roses and are seized by "rose fever," you have a multitude of possibilities: Plant bedding roses throughout the perennial garden as lead plants or install a special rose bed. Even in the smallest gardens and beds there is still room for a standard rose, which can be underplanted beautifully. With more space you can put shrub roses in the lawn or as a hedge. Let scented climbing roses grow over your terrace, sunny wall, or trellis. With their help you can transform boring garden summerhouses or pergolas into lushly blooming visual focal points. Some varieties grow so low, wide, and dense that they can even be used as ground covers.

Always coordinate the colors: Blue and violet go with red, pink, and white roses, while yellow roses are complemented by delicate shades like white, yellow, or silver.

But never forget to remove the spent flowers regularly. Don't put off this burdensome task but devote a few minutes to it daily. Older roses tend to get a little bare in their lower regions. You can prevent this with appropriate pruning or compensate by underplanting with suitable perennials. Roses are hardy to zones 3–9, depending on species and hybrid.

The diversity of roses—there is a right one for every garden.

Climbing and Shrub Roses

Low, Repeat-flowering Roses

Variety Group	Flower Color Flower	Height (in/cm) Of Special Note
'Alexander' Hybrid tea	light vermilion semidouble, fragrant	35/90 Flowers individual
'Allgold' Floribunda	golden-yellow double, fragrant	16–28/40–70 Clustered flowers
'Edelweiss' Floribunda	cream-white double, fragrant	16–24/40–60 Clustered flowers
'Mainaufeuer' Ground-cover rose	blood-red double	20/50 Clustered flowers
'Ponderosa' Floribunda	blood orange semidouble	20/50 Clustered flowers
'Symphony' Hybrid tea	carmine pink double, fragrant	35/90 Flowers individual

Medium-height, Repeat-flowering Roses

'Chaucer' English Rose	delicate pink double, fragrant	39/100 Flowers individual
'Gertrude Jekyll' English Rose	glowing pink double, strongly fragrant	59–71/150–180 Flowers individual
'Gloria Dei' Hybrid tea	golden-yellow with pink densely doubled, fragrant	47/120 Flowers individual
'Heritage' English Rose	delicate pink double, strongly fragrant	47/120 Flowers individual
'Nymphenburg' Shrub rose	orange with pink semidouble, fragrant	59/150 Clustered flowers
'Othello' English Rose	crimson double, strongly fragrant	59/150 Flowers individual

Tall, Repeat-flowering Roses

'Abraham Darby' English Rose	apricot with pink double, fragrant	59–83/150–210 Flowers individual
'Elmshorn' Shrub rose	salmon pink double	59–79/150–200 Clustered flowers
'Goldstern' Climber	deep golden-yellow double	79–118/200–300 Clustered flowers
'Gruss an Heidelberg' Shrub rose	crimson double, fragrant	79–118/200–300 Clustered flowers
'Gruss an Koblenz' Climber	fiery blood-red double	79–118/200–300 Clustered flowers
'Paul's Scarlet Climber' Climber	scarlet semidouble, fragrant	118–158/300–400 Clustered flowers
'Sympathie' Climber	velvety dark-red double, very fragrant	118–158/300–400 Clustered flowers
'Westerland' Shrub rose	golden-yellow with orange semidouble, fragrant	59–70/150–200 Clustered flowers

Climbing Rose
'New Dawn'
Height/Width: up to 13 ft (4m)/
7–13 ft (2–4 m)
Blooms: June–October
Woody plant

▶ **very rewarding variety**

Flowers: Delicate pink-whitish, slightly fragrant, medium-sized (Ø about 2 in [5 cm]), loosely double, situated in thick clusters; rain-fast and self-cleaning, ever-blooming. **Soil:** Nourishing, loamy. **Care:** Train up soft canes on a trellis; in spring apply complete fertilizer when new growth appears and in August give potassium-magnesium fertilizer; in spring take out dead wood and old, crossing, or crowded canes. **Design:** Grow on sunny walls on trellises, let ramble over arbors, pergolas, walls, and fences.

Climbing Rose
'Golden Showers'
Height/Width: 8–15 ft (2–4 m)/
5–10 ft (1–3 m)
Blooms: May–October
Woody plant

▶ **Bright, cheerful, robust variety**

Flowers: Large-sized (Ø 4–5$\frac{1}{2}$ in [10–14 cm]) daffodil yellow, lightly fragrant flowers bloom profusely on this hardy climber. **Soil:** Well-drained, rich loamy soil amended with lots of organic matter. **Care:** Cut back in early spring by one-half and remove old or dead canes. Train up a trellis or wall, making sure that plant has good air circulation; apply a complete fertilizer in early spring and fertilize every 2–3 weeks through mid-August. **Design:** Use to climb on trellis, fences, walls, pergolas, arbors, or other structures; plant has larger thorns so keep it away from narrow garden pathways.

GOOD PARTNERS
Clematis, veronica, campanula, betony

Shrub roses introduce color to the border and provide accents, climbing roses captivate with their cascading wealth of flowers, ground-cover roses suppress weeds.

Small Shrub Rose
'Sommerwind'
Height/Width: 24 in (0.6 m)/ 24 in (0.6 m)
Blooms: June–September
Woody plant

▶ **ideal for garden on a slope**

Flowers: Brilliant pink, then paling, weakly fragrant, medium-sized (Ø 2½in [6 cm]), loosely doubled; clustered; ever-blooming. **Soil:** Nourishing, loamy. **Care:** Complete fertilizer in spring, toward end of summer potassium-magnesium fertilizer; prune back in spring. **Design:** As small groups (1–3 at intervals of 24 in [60 cm]) to stabilize slopes and as ground cover; also in perennial beds with blue-red color schemes; charming as a standard.

Shrub Rose
'Iceberg'
Height/Width: up to 5 ft (1.5 m)/ 3–5 ft (1–1.5 m)
Blooms: June–September
Woody plant

▶ **for pastel-colored beds**

Flowers: White with yellow stamens, sometimes touched with pink, fragrant, medium-sized (Ø 2¾–3 in [7–8 cm]), loosely doubled, clustered, rain-fast and self-cleaning, ever-blooming. **Soil:** Nourishing, loamy. **Care:** Complete fertilizer in spring when new growth appears, potassium-magnesium fertilizer toward end of summer; cut back in spring. **Design:** Beautiful as a tall focal point in pastel-colored beds near a sitting area; harmonizes well with other delicately colored roses.

Shrub Rose
'Lichtkönigen Lucia'
Height/Width: 5 ft (1.5 m)/ 3–5 ft (1–1.5 m)
Blooms: June–September
Woody plant

▶ **beautiful in front of dark hedges**

Flowers: Glowing lemon-yellow to light yellow, lightly fragrant, large (Ø up to 4 in [10 cm]), double, hybrid tea shape, form small clusters, ever-blooming. **Soil:** Nourishing, loamy. **Care:** Apply complete fertilizer in spring when new growth appears, potassium-magnesium fertilizer toward end of summer; cut back in spring. **Design:** Beautiful as specimen and in groups; knockout in front of a background of dark-green shrubs; also attractive in a color-coordinated perennial bed.

GOOD PARTNERS
Blue- and red-flowered perennials and annuals

EXPERT TIP
Blooms lavishly once again in late fall.

GOOD PARTNERS
White- or blue-flowered mediu perennials like campanula, la and evergreen candytuft

Old Roses, English Roses, and Bedding Roses

Centifolia/Cabbage Rose
Rosa centifolia
Height/Width: up to 7 ft (2 m)/
3–5 ft (1–1.5 m)
Blooms: June–August
Woody plant

▶ **descendent of many varieties**

Flowers: Depending on variety, white, silver-pink, pink, or red, strongly fragranced, medium-sized (Ø $2^3/_4$–3 in [7–8 cm]), loose to densely double, sometimes quartered, flowers once but lavishly and for a long time. **Soil:** Nourishing, loamy. **Care:** Apply complete fertilizer in spring, toward summer's end potassium-magnesium fertilizer; only thin out in spring. **Design:** As old species, ideal for cottage garden; also good combined with other roses; pretty as a specimen or in a loose hedge.

English Rose
'Charles Austin'
Height/Width: up to 5 ft (1.5 m)/
3 ft (1 m)
Blooms: June–August
Woody plant

▶ **has a very old-fashioned look**

Flowers: Apricot, later overcast with pink, strongly fragrant, large (Ø $3–3^1/_2$ in [8–9 cm]), cup-shaped, very double, lushly flowering, sporadic later flowering. **Soil:** Nourishing, loamy. **Care:** Apply complete fertilizer in spring, potassium-magnesium fertilizer toward summer's end; thin in spring. **Design:** An upright, bushy shrub rose that makes a striking focal point in the background of the bed; also in front of hedges or among lower roses.

Floribunda Rose
'Gruss an Aachen'
Height/Width: up to 20 in (0.5 m)/
up to 20 in (0.5 m)
Blooms: June–September
Woody plant

▶ **very old-fashioned flowers**

Flowers: Cream-white, yellowish to pink overcast in center, slightly fragrant, large (Ø up to 4 in [10 cm]), densely doubled, in clusters, flowers often and lavishly. **Soil:** Nourishing, loamy. **Care:** Apply complete fertilizer in spring, potassium-magnesium fertilizer toward summer's end; cut back in spring. **Design:** A bedding rose best suited to the cottage garden; thrives best in less sunny situations, not in blazing sun; good in combination with pastel-colored roses or perennials.

EXPERT TIP
*Varieties: 'Muscosa' (pink, double),
'...ristata' (pink, double, very fragrant)*

GOOD PARTNERS
*Blue-violet clematis, lavender
as underplanting*

The double, usually fragrant flowers of the old roses and the English roses have much old-fashioned charm. Bedding roses look stiffer and more stately.

Floribunda Rose
'Queen Elizabeth'
Height/Width: 3–6 ft (1–1.8 m)/ about 3 ft (1 m)
Blooms: June–September
Woody plant

▶ **effect is stiff but elegant**

Flowers: Salmon pink, then lightening to bright pink, fragrant, large (Ø 3–4 in [8–10 cm]), loosely double, cup-shaped, in clusters on long stems, repeat-flowering. **Soil:** Nourishing, loamy. **Care:** Apply complete fertilizer in spring, toward summer's end potassium-magnesium fertilizer; cut back in spring. **Design:** Because of its somewhat formal effect, do not mix haphazardly with other perennials but place in its own, color-coordinated rose bed; also suitable for the front yard.

Floribunda Rose
'Edelweiss'
Height/Width: 16 in (0.4 m)/ 16 in (0.4 m)
Blooms: June–September
Woody plant

▶ **very sweet and delicate**

Flowers: Cream-white, from cream yellow buds, slightly fragrant, medium-sized (Ø 2–2³/₄ in [5–7 cm]), quite double, in clusters, ever-blooming. **Soil:** Nourishing, loamy. **Care:** Apply complete fertilizer in spring, potassium-magnesium fertilizer toward summer's end; in fall hill and cover with branches; cut back in spring. **Design:** As bedding rose can be combined with red roses for contrast or harmonized with pale-pink and yellow roses; choose pastel shades for neighboring perennials.

Hybrid Tea
'Erotica'
Height/Width: 32 in (0.8 m)/ 16–20 in (0.4–0.5 m)
Blooms: June–September
Woody plant

▶ **intense color**

Flowers: Velvety dark-red, strongly fragrant, large (Ø up to 4 in [10 cm]), quite double, single flowers on long stems, weather-fast, continuous flowering. **Soil:** Nourishing, loamy. **Care:** Apply complete fertilizer in spring when new growth appears, at summer's end potassium-magnesium fertilizer; hill before first frost and cover with branches; cut back in spring. **Design:** As bedding rose looks best with other roses or as eye-catcher among lower perennials and ornamental grasses; also very good cut flower.

GOOD PARTNERS
Speedwell, snow-in-summer, mouse-ear chickweed, thyme

EXPERT TIP
The flowers hold for a markedly long time.

GOOD PARTNERS
Monkshood, myrtle, lavender, salvia

Climbing Plants

These belong in every garden to the extent that it is possible. Climbing plants need very little space because they grow up. They can ornament, establish distinctive accents, and also conceal things that are unsightly.

The classic assignment for climbing plants is the greening of the house. But in this case there are some points that need to be considered: Evergreen ivy certainly does develop very dense curtains; however, its aerial roots can invade cracks in a wall and damage it. If you want to avoid this risk, you should choose species that don't form aerial roots but pull themselves upward by their shoots on supports. Establish these at a distance of about 4 in (10 cm) from the house or property wall. If the wall belongs to a neighbor, you should ask permission first.

Apart from that, you can green all the tall constructed elements in your garden with climbing plants: arbors and trellises, garden houses and pergolas. Don't merely plant vines to overgrow unattractive sights but also use them solely as design elements (see pages 158 and 168).

The Right Choice

While some vines have an attractive appearance thanks to their foliage, others only become fully effective when they bloom. Vigorously growing vines with dense foliage offer good privacy and are especially suited for greening of summerhouses and pergolas, while many exuberantly flowering forms don't have view-blocking leaves. These belong on arbors and gates, trellises, or pillars, providing color and height at the back of the border. If you have an old garden with tall, not too densely crowned trees, you can let climbing roses, clematis, or silver lace vine (very aggressive!) climb up them. This looks very natural and lends the garden much atmosphere.

Vines can provide lush flowering in the smallest space.

Foliage Plants for Walls and Fences

Kiwi
Actinidia chinensis
Height/Width: up to 33 ft (10 m)/ up to 16 ft (5 m)
Blooms: May–June
Summer-green shrub

▶ **twiner, edible fruit**

Flowers: White (Ø 1–2 in [3–5 cm]), from which, in November, in protected warmer locations, when a male and female plant are planted, edible brown, hairy fruits ripen. **Soil:** Well-drained, not too dry, acid (pH 4–6). **Care:** As a twiner, needs support; for a good fruit harvest the side shoots are cut back in winter and pinched out in summer, with superfluous runners also removed; if the plant is only grown for decoration, no pruning is necessary. **Design:** Beautiful on a trellis or on the pergola. Extremely vigorous grower. **Zone:** 7–11.

Ivy
Hedera helix
Height/Width: up to 66 ft (20 m)/ up to 49 ft (15 m)
Blooms: September–October
Evergreen shrub

▶ **self-climber**

Flowers: Only on old plants, insignificant, green-yellow, from which the next year develop poisonous black berries. **Soil:** Any normal, fresh garden soil. **Care:** Tie up the first shoots after planting; afterwards the ivy will climb by means of its aerial roots alone; fertilize organically in spring; cut back if necessary. **Design:** With intact plaster, the best wall greening for shady surfaces; also useful as ground cover. **Zone:** 5–9.

Silver Lace Vine, China Fleece Vine
Polygonum aubertii
Height/Width: up to 40 ft (12 m)/ up to 13 ft (4 m)
Blooms: June–August
Summer-green shrub

▶ **rampant twiner**

Flowers: White, in loose panicles (Ø about 5–8 mm), strongly fragrant, from which develop tiny winged seeds that are carried by the wind and can be burdensome in surrounding areas. **Soil:** Damp, otherwise undemanding. **Care:** Provide stable support (sturdy wires, trellis), water plentifully, especially during dry spells and in a location under an overhanging roof; cut back as necessary. **Design:** Beautiful on walls, arbors, pergolas, garden houses, fences. **Zone:** 4–9.

EXPERT TIP
Varieties: 'Wilson' is a cultivar hardy to zone 4. 'Argenteo-variegate' is a variegated white.

GOOD PARTNERS
The spotted dead nettle is an ideal underplanting.

Some of the green plants here are self-climbers, some need supports. All form a dense green coating with their leaves.

Wintercreeper
Euonymus fortunei
Height/Width: up to 10 ft (3 m)/ 7 ft (2 m)
Blooms: May–June
Evergreen shrub

▶ **self-climber**

Flowers: Greenish-white, very rare, but then also from August, 8 mm-wide greenish-reddish, poisonous fruits. **Soil:** Normal, fresh garden soil. **Care:** Mulch after planting; water plentifully during dry spells; if possible, do not prune; disturbing shoots can be carefully taken out. **Design:** The wintercreeper is not only a good ground cover but it can also climb by means of its aerial rootlets as high as 10 ft (3 m) on objects that are not too smooth; less vigorously growing varieties are suitable for container culture. **Zone:** 4–9.

Pipevine, Dutchman's Pipe
Aristolochia durior
Height/Width: 26–33 ft (8–10 m)/ up to 26 ft (8 m)
Blooms: June–August
Summer-green shrub

▶ **large-leaved twiner**

Flowers: Yellow-green outside, purple-brown inside trumpet-trap flowers, which lure flies. **Soil:** Humusy and fresh; must not dry out. **Care:** Fertilize with compost in spring; water plentifully, especially during dry spells; cover with branches as protection against frost. **Design:** The large, heart-shaped leaves, up to 12 in (30 cm) long remain long on the branch; give an open garden house an almost tropical look and grow so thickly that curious glances are thwarted. **Zone:** 4–8.

Woodbine
Parthenocissus species
Height/Width: up to 49 ft (15 m)/ up to 33 ft (10 m)
Blooms: June–July
Summer-green shrub

▶ **creeper, self-climber**

Flowers: Insignificant, from which develop, beginning in September, blue-black fruits 5–7 mm wide. **Soil:** Any not-too-dry garden soil. **Care:** Fertilize with organic fertilizer in spring; *P. quinquefolia* (Virginia creeper) climbs primarily with twining creepers, is rewarding for trellises, and should be tied at first; *P. tricuspidata*, on the other hand, clings with disks without help to any not too smooth surface. **Design:** Ideal for facades and walls; brilliant crimson fall coloring, starting in September, in sufficient sun. **Zone:** 3–9.

EXPERT TIP
Pictured is the variety 'Emerald 'n Gold' (pale-yellow leaf margins)

EXPERT TIP
Pictured is the five-leaved P. quinquefolia (Virginia creeper)

Trailing Cascades of Flowers

Honeysuckle, Woodbine
Lonicera periclymenum
Height/Width: 8–40 ft (2–12 m)/
up to 10 ft (3 m)
Blooms: May–July
Summer-green shrub

▶ **fast-growing twiner**

Flowers: Long tubes, depending on variety, pure-white and purplish-pink to yellowish-white and purple (1$1/2$–1$3/4$ in [4–4.5 cm] long), with strong evening fragrance, from which form poisonous, dark-red berries (Ø 7–8 mm) in August. **Soil:** Any garden soil. **Care:** Plant with robust supports such as wires, mesh, or wooden trellises; mulch and fertilize with organic fertilizer in spring; occasionally thin older bushes. Prune back in early summer for more summer blooms. **Design:** Pretty on walls, sturdy fences, arbors, and pergolas; also grows up trees. **Zone:** 5–9.

Climbing Hydrangea
Hydrangea anomala ssp. *petiolaris*
Height/Width: up to 33 ft (10 m)/
up to 20 ft (6 m)
Blooms: June–July
Summer-green shrub

▶ **robust self-climber**

Flowers: White (Ø 1 in [3 cm], in 6–8 in [15–20 cm] -wide umbrella panicles), delicately fragrant. **Soil:** Fresh to moist, deeply cultivated, nutrient-rich, also alkaline. **Care:** Lead the shoots of young plant up; after it grows it climbs with aerial roots on walls and also on trellises and trees; fertilize in spring; if possible, do not prune; water regularly during dry spells in summer. **Design:** As one of the few shade-tolerant, flowering climbers it is well suited for greening not very sunny areas. **Zone:** 5–7.

Winter Jasmine
Jasminum nudiflorum
Height/Width: up to 10 ft (3 m)/
about 7 ft (2 m)
Blooms: December–April
Summer-green shrub

▶ **spreading climber**

Flowers: Yellow, often red on the outside (Ø about 1 in [2.5 cm]), appear before leaves, not fragrant. **Soil:** Well-drained, fresh, nutrient-rich, also alkaline. **Care:** As a thin-tendriled spreading climber needs a support for climbing, preferably a trellis; also water in winter in frost-free weather; thin out densely grow-ing shoots; cut back older ones. **Design:** Grows on wall trellises, garden houses, and pergolas; the branches can also trail artistically over supporting walls, steps, or landings. **Zone:** 6–9.

EXPERT TIP
Relatives: Italian woodbine
(L. caprifolium), *flowers yellow-white*

GOOD PARTNERS
Lush summer bloomers
like clematis

Luxuriantly blooming climbers only rarely provide privacy, of course, but they transform walls and supports to an overflowing sea of flowers.

Large-Flowered Clematis

Clematis hybrids, shown: 'Jackmannii'
Height/Width: up to 10 ft (3 m)/
up to 7 ft (2 m)
Blooms: July–August (Sept)
Summer-green shrub

▶ **large-flowered twiner**

Flowers: Depending on variety, white, pink, crimson, purple, violet, sky- to dark-blue to purple-blue, also bicolors or striped (Ø 2–4 in [5–10 cm]). **Soil:** Fresh, humus-rich, alkaline. **Care:** Fertilize with organic fertilizer in spring; according to the requirements of the variety, cut back regularly; during dry spells water thoroughly. **Design:** Ideal for terrace trellises, pergolas, and house entries; together with other, color-coordinated clematis or climbing roses; shade at the bottom with ground covers. **Zone:** most are hardy to zones 3–8, but a few are only hardy to zones 6–7.

Clematis Montana

Clematis montana, shown: 'Rubens'
Height/Width: up to 33 ft (10 m)/
up to 16 ft (5 m)
Blooms: May–June
Summer-green shrub

▶ **luxuriantly flowering twiner**

Flowers: Depending on variety, white, pink, to lilac-pink (Ø $1/2$–$2^1/2$ in [2–6 cm]). **Soil:** Fresh, humus-rich, well-drained, alkaline. **Care:** Train young plants onto supports; suitable are wires, wooden frames, or wire mesh; cover against late frosts; apply organic fertilizer in spring; water during prolonged dry spells; no pruning necessary; cut out too-dense growth after flowering. **Design:** This wild species is ideal for natural gardens, for greening passageways and pergolas. **Zone:** 6–10.

Wisteria

Wisteria sinensis
Height/Width: up to 49 ft (15 m)/
up to 33 ft (10 m)
Blooms: April–May
Summer-green shrub

▶ **rope-like, binding twiner**

Flowers: Light-blue to violet, also white varieties (Ø 1 in [2.5 cm], in 6–12-in [15–30-cm] -long clusters). **Soil:** Fresh, well-drained, nutrient-rich, acid to neutral. **Care:** It's essential to use sturdy supports such as strong wire; use lime-free fertilizer in spring; cutting back after flowering recommended; water during prolonged dry spells. **Design:** Beautiful on pergolas, arbors, house fronts, but don't allow near drainpipes or gutters, which it can crush. **Zone:** 4–9.

EXPERT TIP
Varieties: 'Dr. Ruppel' (white and rose), 'Rouge Cardinal' (dark-red)

GOOD PARTNERS
Golden-chain tree (laburnum) with its yellow flower clusters

Designing Gardens

Painting with Flowers

The goal of any design is a garden that appeals to the mind and spirit. Relax and let yourself be guided by your instincts.

We all possess a feeling for the beautiful even if the idea varies widely among individuals. With design it is a matter of activating this sense and "painting" the garden like a picture. A painter will decide on a motif, compose the picture, and then put in the colors. The same goes for garden design: The "motif" is the type of garden and the picture composition corresponds to the arrangement and form of the garden. Finally, colors of foliage and flowers determine the mood of the garden. Pictures/gardens can excite or calm the viewer, induce meditation, or have a joyous or exciting effect. If you design your garden as an expression of personality, it should be right for you and you should feel comfortable in it.

How Do I Start?

Keep in mind: A landscape architect has been through a course of study and is working as a professional. So you shouldn't expect to score a big hit in your own garden design right at the very beginning. As a layperson, you do have the advantage of not being bound by strict, formal rules as the professional is; therefore your garden can have a far more spontaneous and lively effect.

▶ First plan a single bed. If that succeeds, all to the good—if not, then change it until the bed form, play of colors, and growth forms harmonize well.

▶ Install large, solid elements (pergolas, arbors, large hedges as dividers) cautiously at first; live with it a while, and only then start building in new elements.

Time is on your side anyway, for over the years gardens develop more charm: Trees and shrubs reach their final size, the beds establish themselves, and not least, you become a skilled gardener.

Even the smallest area will accommodate a multitude of green and flowering plants.

Color, Shape, and Space

On the following pages you will find an introduction to the "art" of garden design. The main point here is less to introduce you to "finished" gardens—given the numbers of the varieties of possible garden situations, that would be an undertaking doomed to failure—than it is to provide a basic overview of the use of particular design elements.

Color

Probably the colors used have the most direct influence on the effect of a garden. Colors express moods and must therefore be used purposefully. Also the location plays a decisive role in the effects colors have.
▶ Light colors are accentuated even more by sunshine; on the other hand, they also illuminate dark areas.
▶ Dark colors look dull in shade; they need sunlight to show them off.
▶ Always build your beds around a basic color or a combination of contrasts and choose the other colors to go with it. It's best to follow the color wheel for this.
▶ Complementary colors (yellow/blue or red/green) create rich contrasts.
▶ Lively color triads are created by contrasts of yellow, red, and blue.

▶ Depending on the color group, beds designed with shading tones can be lively (yellow to orange) or restful (blue to violet).
▶ The colors yellow, orange, and red provide warmth.
▶ Cool colors are blue, turquoise, and green.

Shapes

Beds and growth forms create frames or backgrounds—they present the colors and move them into the right light.

For design purposes, a differentiation is made between large forms, like lawns and bed areas, and the growth forms of the plants.
▶ Square, circular, or hexagonal beds appear quiet and static.
▶ The related rectangular and oval forms are neutral.

The Color Wheel

The colors of the rainbow are placed next to one another on the color wheel, thus providing guidance in combining colors.

▶ All slanting, scalloped, or narrow surfaces bring movement into the garden.

Thus, a careful choice of growth forms, too, is highly recommended, because most perennials only bloom for a few weeks; after they are finished, the leaves and growth forms must create the effect. Bridge over the rest of the season by using plants that are hemispherical, columnar, or have grasslike foliage. They provide interest and are often the only possible design tool for shaded areas.

Spaces

Gardens that the viewer can take in at a glance are boring. Subdividing the garden at the beginning creates "rooms," which enclose and shut out. Rooms and subdivisions make the viewer curious about what lies concealed behind them and provides suspense. This does not mean designing the "walls" of the rooms compactly in the form of dense hedges or walls. A single shrub or tree, a low, flowering hedge, corridors in the form of arches and pergolas or trellises separate and connect at the same time.

Above all, when the garden is closed off by means of an external frame (wall, bordering structures,

Green by itself need not be boring if various growth and leaf forms are artfully combined.

high hedge), it provides an internal subdivision for spacious depth. Don't miss an opportunity to subdivide, for it provides interesting possibilities that make the garden more complex and exciting.

Color Creates Mood

Yellow	Light, glowing, warm, makes neighboring colors appear darker
Orange	Mixed color; strong, lively, warm
Red	Warm; light-red shades have a pastel-like effect, gentle; dark-red shades calm, make neighboring colors appear brighter
Violet	Mixed color; cool
Blue	Cool, calming; visually broadens the bed
Green	Calming, mediating; ideal background
White	Neutral, mediating; ideal in front of dark background or in shade
Silver/gray	Neutral, mediating; ideal in pastel combinations

Appealing Flower Color Combinations

Information in Brief

Complementary Colors

Yellow-Blue:
> Achillea, monkshood (see picture)
> Narcissi, crocus
> Yellow loosestrife, delphinium

Red-Green:
> Cardinal flower, castor bean
> (see picture)
> Red salvia, lady's-mantle (foliage)

Color Triad

Yellow-Red-Blue:
> Gloriosa daisy, nicotiana, salvia
> (see picture)
> Alyssum, soapwort, campanulas

Orange-Violet-Light-Green:
> Marigolds/lavender/lady's mantle
> in bloom

Lively Tone-Shading

Yellow-Orange:
> Gloriosa daisies, marigolds
> (see picture)
> Mullein, daylilies

Quiet Tone-Shading

Rose-Violet:
> Salvia, daisies, cranesbill,
> astilbe (see picture)

Lilac-Blue:
> Moss pink, horned viola
> Tall campanulas (varieties),
> delphinium

Complementary Colors

Complementary colors occur opposite each other on the color wheel. Such color combinations have the effect of rich contrast and excitement, since the colors mutually enhance and intensify one another. White, as the third color in complementary beds, tones down the contrast somewhat. The yellow-blue combination (pictured above) creates high tension, while the red-green combination (pictured below) awakens rather quiet associations.

Color Triads

Designing "colorful" beds is one of the most difficult tasks for the gardener. They are only successful when at least three colors of flowers are visible at the same time (color triad), but then they look especially cheerful and lively. You can achieve a strong color triad with yellow, red, and blue. Triads in pastel (orange, light-violet, light-green) produce an airy-light mood.

Mediate with green foliage and sparingly introduced white.

Full of contrast or tone-on-tone—interesting beds need a color theme; otherwise the result is busy confusion.

Lively Tone-Shading

With beds in which the colors are shaded (blended color), you achieve homogeneous moods. Such beds are lovely to look at; they also brighten up dark summer days with their colors. But color gradations are only effective when you limit yourself to a single basic color (yellow to orange; dark orange to red).

Quiet Tone-Shading

Blues shading to violet have a very calming effect. The eye can sweep over such a bed and the spirit find release from the stress of the ordinary workday. Frame such beds with calming shades of green (grass, hedges, shrubs) used as separators and backgrounds. White—possibly in similar flower forms—mediates among the various shades of blue.

Silver Beds

A bed is ordinarily planned for the season of the flowers. Here silver- and gray-leaved plants, which also create their effect beyond the flowering season, are combined with white flowers.

Silver- and gray-leaved plants such as artemisia, lamb's ear, and Russian Sage are easily available. Plants with light-blue, pink, or white flowers all go extremely well with gray and silver.

EXPERT TIP
Pastels belong in the foreground.

CROSS-REFERENCES
Establishing beds pages 28–29
Plant portraits pages 78–145

Play with Form

Information in Brief

Narrow, tall Perennials

Mullein (*Verbascum*)
Evening primrose
Giant allium
Delphinium
Yucca

Pillar-shaped Shrubs

Pillar yew
Juniper

Spherical Plants

Clipped box
Lady's-mantle
Hosta
Heaths and heathers
Lavender
Cranesbill

Fan-shaped Plants

Ferns
Grasses
Day Lilies

The Wavy Bed
When you lay out a bed for the first time, you should position the plants by color first. If you then choose cushion- and clump-forming plants of about the same height, it results in a wavy bed like the one shown here (rose-colored daylilies, ruby-red mountain fleece, lilac, woodruff). It has a certain formality, but the effect, even when the flowers are not in bloom, is very lively, for the eye does not rest on a flat plane but "wanders" across the upper surfaces.

Wavy Beds with Exclamation Points
Wavy beds are even more lively when they are punctuated by occasional narrow and tall perennials (here by the yellow-flowered desert-candle in the midst of iris and nepeta). They draw the eye upward, producing a certain tension. The contrast derives from the different growth forms and not from an additional color. In designing such beds it is not a matter of the absolute heights but of the relationship of the lower plants to the higher ones.

Growth forms are just as important to design in the garden as colors, for they create the ongoing basic framework of the beds.

Contrast of Form and Color

Differing growth forms are further accentuated by the form and color of their leaves. In this pure-green planting for a shady area the contrast results from the compact, hemispherical growth form of the white-variegated hosta, the massive linden-green leaves of the rodgersia, and the feathery, light-green fronds of the fern. Planted for their shape, grasslike leaves (e.g., ornamental grasses, day lilies) that spread in a fan go outstandingly well with cushion plants. While the cushions suggest compactness, grass fans "open" the bed.

A Little Formality Doesn't Hurt

Particularly in the small garden, there is some justification for the formal pruning of small-leaved woody plants. Two boxwoods pruned to spheres and placed as a pair draw the eye through a particular area of the garden as if down an avenue. Also, in cottage and kitchen gardens and potagers (shown here, a spring arrangement), boxwoods pruned into severely formal shapes provide a contrast to the lush forms and colors of the beds.

Beds with Mixed Forms

Give your imagination free reign in such beds: High and low, bushy and narrow, delicate and massive plants should crowd in on all sides and accentuate one another. This style requires flower colors that are assembled according to color triads. However, when you are drawing up the planting plan, pay special to heights and spacing, so that the individual plants remain visible and the stronger ones don't overwhelm the weaker.

EXPERT TIP
Plant small shrubs in the bed as focal points.

CROSS-REFERENCES
Establishing beds pages 28–29
Color designing pages 152–153

Bed Shapes

Information in Brief

Peninsular Beds

Arc diameter of at least
5 ft (150 cm)

Lawn Area Dipping into Borders

Arc diameter of at least
10 ft (300 cm)

Island Beds

Surface area at least
22–32 ft^2 (2–3 m^2)

Raised Beds

Surface area at least
11–22 ft^2 (1–2 m^2)

Bed Edging

Planking:
Rustic, harmonizes with
cottage-garden plants
Dry walls of natural stone:
Natural garden
Walls of frostproof brick:
Formal, austere; strong
contrast to lush planting

Straight-edged Borders

Large lawn areas do not make a small garden appear any larger. A homogeneous green surface does not offer the eye any focal points, the glance glides automatically to the bordering areas of the garden. In this case, design the borders to be especially rich in variety. Even a single small tree or larger shrub that is placed assymetrically in the lawn contributes to a varied garden landscape.

Curving Beds

Whenever the garden situation permits it, choose a curving bed shape. Lawn areas that sweep into borders create depth, while peninsular beds reaching into the lawn offer more interest and subdivide the garden.

Establishing a bed is expensive and imprints the picture of the garden for years. So play with a few possibilities on paper first.

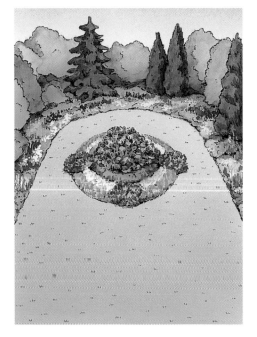  

The Island Bed in the Lawn

In larger yards or in lawns that are less intensively used, put a bed in the lawn. The green "frame" shows it off especially well. Shifted into the foreground, an island bed with pastel-colored flowers creates spacious depth in the garden. In putting together the plants, try for a picture that is as harmonious as possible but also rich in variety.

Raised Beds

Flowers are presented especially interestingly in raised beds: Let the plants grow down in cascades over the edge, or structure "graduated" beds like ponds in which the water flows from basin to basin.

Since the plants remain enclosed in a relatively small space, raised beds are very easy to care for.

The Edge Planting of the Bed

The transition between lawn and bed requires special attention. With low-growing plants this border area is structured flowingly, which can easily turn into boredom. Therefore it is better to place some larger perennials along the edge of the bed now and again, which grow above the lawn and "break" the flowing transition. Still more impressive is the effect of strengthening the "outer frame" (the green of the lawn) with an "inner frame" of similar edging plants.

EXPERT TIP
*Restrict yourself to
one shape of bed.*

CROSS-REFERENCES
*Establishing beds pages 28–29
Designing beds pages 162–167*

Creating Rooms

Information in Brief

Privacy

Trellises (woodbine)
Pergolas (silver lace vine,
Dutchman's pipevine)
Walkways (wisteria)
Hedges

Open Partitions

Trellises (roses, clematis)
Pergolas (honeysuckle,
clematis, roses)
Walkways (roses, clematis,
winter jasmine)
Arches and gates (bare or
with growing things)

Focal Points

Pergolas (bare or with
growing things)
Walkways (roses, clematis,
wisteria)

Passages

Arches, gates, walkways
(bare or with growing
things)

Terrace with Trellis
You can use a trellis to shield your
sitting area on the terrace from
curious glances. If possible place
the trellis so that it both fulfills
its function of privacy and produces
sunny and shady areas on your
terrace.

A Rose Arch as a Room Divider
We perceive gateways unconsciously
as connecting elements, so a single
rose arch in the middle of a meadow
is in the wrong place. On the other
hand, it is perfect as a fragrant
passageway.

Rose arches draw the eye through
the arching shape and with their
flowers provide a splendid focal point.

Even in small gardens, create separated areas that reveal themselves slowly.

Foliage Walkways as Room Dividers

Foliage walkways with flowering vines form extraordinarily effective space dividers. As architectural elements that are accentuated even more by leaves and flowers, they set strong accents and add value to even the smallest gardens.

Plan the walkway so that it can be seen through from the main sitting area.

Since the eye is directed through the walkway, like an avenue, to a particular spot, you should accent this focal point with a special plant, a bench, or a sculpture.

Vine-covered Pergolas

With a free-standing pergola you create a focal point and with sufficient size (10 × 13 ft [3 × 4 m]) you gain an additional, shady sitting area in the garden. Since pergolas protect the area behind them from view, they also create the perfect space dividers at the same time.

Much more "transparent" is the effect of the single-beam pergola, which can be arranged horizontally, at an angle, or lengthwise—these separate without obstructing the view.

Hedges as Room Dividers

Separating one part of the yard completely from another is only possible in larger gardens. Then design a hedge, but make it a green work of art, a so-called "tapestry hedge."

A tapestry hedge consists of evergreen components (yew or other conifers) and deciduous shrubs (hornbeam, beech, or red-leaved copper beech). Interrupt the partition created by such hedges with a generous gateway.

In smaller yards a hedge is, as a rule, used as a boundary to the yard and offers privacy from the outside.

EXPERT TIP
Use construction materials for pergolas and arbors. Decorative lattice work on an arbor adds more ornamental value.

CROSS-REFERENCES
Sitting areas in the garden pages 178–179
Climbing plants pages 140–145

Design Suggestions

**The last step in garden design consists
of transferring the theoretical concept
to the concrete garden situation.**

Many famous gardeners have written thick volumes about garden design. We know about antique, medieval, renaissance, and baroque gardens. In more recent times volumes have appeared about all kinds of specialized gardens. For the beginner, it is scarcely possible to survey this jumble of information. It would exceed the framework of this book to go into all possible garden situations exhaustively. However, there are certain basic elements in any garden with which even the novice should be familiar.

The Basic Elements of a Garden

Besides the lawn, which belongs in any garden, the beds and trees and shrubs are primary in determining the character of a garden.

▶ Every bed must be planned according to its location, for shade or sun, wetness or dryness determine the choice of plants. A sunny bed, for instance, will look quite different from a bed in the shade. Be clear about where you want to put your bed and then draw up a planting diagram.

▶ The third dimension of the garden, the height, is shaped by the trees and shrubs. Whether you want to plant one or more trees, a shrubbery border hedge, or only a single shrub is a very personal decision. However, consider that all woody plants increase in size over the course of the years.

▶ Green-clad walls or constructions like foliage walkways and pergolas also provide height.

▶ Skillfully planted, planters and tubs are an elegant opportunity to design additional "ready-made" gardens. Singly or assembled in groups they provide immediate color.

▶ Herb spirals represent kitchen gardens "in miniature." They look pretty and provide the kitchen with fresh seasoning and medicinal herbs.

▶ Paths and sitting areas complete the garden picture.

*In this garden, lawn and plants
are skillfully used to link sitting
area, garden pond, and house.*

Garden Design— Step by Step

Every good garden begins in someone's head. The more precisely you know what you want where, the more easily you can translate your dreams into practice.

The Garden Plan

While a new house is being constructed, the owner has much time to wait. Bridge this time by developing a garden plan. Use the property survey or the architect's plan of your property as a model; these already show the position of the house.

▶ Enlarge the garden area to about $8^1/_2$ by 14 inches (make a number of copies or use transparent drawing paper laid over the ground plan).

▶ Next subdivide the area grossly according to the intended uses. How large should the lawn be? Do you plan a fence, a narrow pruned hedge, or a wide shrub border along the boundary? Would you like to create a sitting area, a pergola, or a leafy walkway? Is the garden big enough for a separate vegetable garden or potager?

▶ Take into consideration the neighbors' trees and buildings, as well as views into the landscape. If you try to include these elements in the area, the possible quickly separates out from the impossible.

Now comes the most difficult part of planning, the precise area determination of the basic elements in the ground plan. To do this you can either start with known elements or plan everything around a pathway system.

Planning with Solid Elements

When you want to erect a walkway, pergola, or a sitting area, you should proceed in the following way:

▶ Cut the areas of the elements in question from a piece of cardboard, keeping the cutouts in the correct relative scale.

▶ Move these outlines around on the plan and back and forth until you have found a satisfactory solution.

▶ Then finally draw the element onto the plan.

▶ Now arrange the other components of the garden (lawns, beds, paths, water areas) relative to the stationary one(s) you have already determined.

Garden Ornaments

Every garden can be made even more beautiful by appropriate garden ornaments—sculptures, containers, figurines.

Planning with a Pathway System

Paths are uniting linear, straight, or wavy elements that make each part of the yard accessible. When planning, it is unimportant whether you use firm flagstone paths, gravel, or "only" lawn as a pathway system.

▶ Consider, however, that regularly used stretches must be stable and nonslip.

▶ Straight paths have a more formal, severe effect than curving, looping paths.

▶ Paths that are partially concealed from the eye appear especially charming. Let them curve behind large shrubs or shrubbery beds or lead you through green foliage passageways or arches.

▶ Orient the other garden elements to the network of paths.

▶ Be careful to keep a consistent picture: Naturally, curving paths need a correlation in form of rounded or curving bed outlines, while straight paths are better looking between formally structured beds.

The Planting Plan

The planting of beds and construction of garden structures constitute the last step in planning.

• Enlarge the now-established bed areas according to the size of the garden freehand or with a photocopier, so that you have enough space to write in the desired plants.

Such an artfully designed garden demands a skillful plan and a great deal of maintenance.

▶ In the Choosing Plants section, the ultimate width is given for each of the plants. You can simply use a compass to transfer this to the paper (thus automatically giving you the number of plants needed).

▶ But above all, keep in mind the end height trees and shrubs will attain.

▶ Explore the different possibilities on paper.

You can only achieve a garden paradise step by step. This means doing things in the proper order, recognizing basic design principles, and planning a garden that fits with the house and surroundings.

How Many Plants per Square Foot?

Tall perennials (39–79 in [100–200 cm])	2–5
Medium-tall perennials (20–35 in [50–90 cm])	5–9
Low perennials (8–16 in [20–40 cm])	7–12
Ground covers	10–15
Bulbs	12–25

EXPERT TIP
*Transparent graph paper
is ideal for planning.*

CROSS-REFERENCES
*Garden design pages 148–179
Choosing plants pages 78–145*

Sunny Island in a Sea of Grass

Information in Brief

Tools

Spade or spading fork
Trowel

Materials

Humus

Planting Times

Fall:
Bulbs, corms, and tubers
for spring flowers
Spring:
Perennials (develop in
subsequent years)
from April:
Sow annuals or plant (new
every year)
from May:
Dahlia tubers (new every
year)

Time Expenditure

3–4 hours for about
33–54 ft² (4–5 m²)

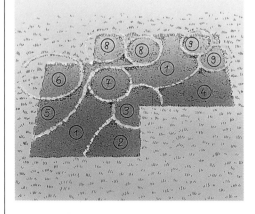

Planning, Preparation, Planting Plan

The bed is laid out some way away from the sitting area, since its colors also work at a distance because of the high signal effect. Draw the shape of the bed (square 59 × 5 9 in [150 × 150 cm]) and rectangle 39 × 79 in [100 × 200 cm]) to the correct scale on a piece of graph paper and put in the desired plants. Prepare the bed for planting and sprinkle the planting area with sand.

Planting Perennials

Begin by planting the tall plants in the center of the bed. Try to walk in the bed as little as possible so as not to compact the soil (put down a board, see drawing). Don't make the mistake of putting the plants too close together—a newly laid out bed should look "empty"—by the following year, at the latest, the growing plants will have filled in all the gaps.

This bed sparkles in the hot colors of summer.
The green grass frame effectively underlines
the shades of orange and yellow.

Foreground Planting

The low-growing plants are put in after the tall plants. The annuals in the foreground are offered by many nurseries as started plants. This is, of course, somewhat more expensive than sowing your own, but it saves work and disappointment. As soon as you have gotten some experience in the course of your "garden life," you should have no qualms about daring to sow your own.

The Finished Bed

The bed laid out according to the plan on the opposite page unfurls its glory from June to September. In the fall, plant the preceding year's bulbs, corms, and tubers in place of the annuals, and then your bed will already begin to bloom in the spring. The golden-yellow gloriosa daisy (7) forms the center, and behind it stands the somewhat taller goldenrod (8), whose long inflorescences make a good contrast. The tall, red-violet lupines (6), make a striking point of focus with their color and size. In the right-hand section of the bed, two day lilies (9) with narrow, grasslike leaves and large flowers provide an accent. The band of heleniums (1) that runs diagonally through the bed serves to link and generate interest. In front of it annuals (gazanias, 2; marigolds, 3; zinnias, 4) provide a transition from the green of the lawn to the bed, while the single dahlias (5) bridge between foreground and lupines.

The various growth and leaf forms provide for a picture rich in variety.

EXPERT TIP
The bed can also be laid out with curving edges.

CROSS-REFERENCES
Establishing a bed pages 28–29
Planting perennials pages 42–43

Renovating a Shady Bed

Information in Brief

Tools

Spade or spading fork
Trowel

Materials

Humus

Planting Times

Woody plants:
 Fall or spring
Perennials:
 Spring or late summer
Ferns:
 Spring

Time Expenditure

4–5 hours for about 65–75 ft² (6–7 m²)

The Existing Bed

The bed is situated in front of a wall, which provides shade from late morning on. The variegated wintercreeper and a group of astilbes and of goatsbeard are shade-tolerant, so they stay in the bed. The hazel basically also tolerates some shade, but it easily grows too large. It should, along with all the other ornamental plants and weeds, be removed. Design the present edge to be somewhat more "swinging," perhaps in the form of two sweeping arcs.

Structuring the Wall Surface

Next attach a trellis to the wall (ask permission of your neighbor if the wall doesn't belong to you). Plant ivy behind the wintercreeper, and tie the first shoots firmly to the trellis (later ivy will climb by means of its aerial roots). Since the wintercreeper has colored leaves, a plain green ivy variety is recommended here (with green shrubs, correspondingly, use variegated ivy). The rest of the wall (use a trellis!) is planted with Virginia creeper.

This suggestion for renovating a shady bed includes plants already present; naturally you can also start the bed from scratch.

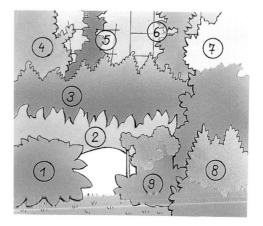

Planting Plan

1 Hosta (*Hosta* species or hybrids in green or green-and-white), two plants.
2 Hart's tongue fern (*Phyllitis scolopendrium*).
3 Male fern (*Dryopteris felix-mas*), about five plants.
4 Wintercreeper (*Euonymus fortunei*, variegated, tall variety), one plant.
5 Ivy (*Hedera helix*, green variety), one plant.
6 Virginia creeper (*Parthenocissus quinquefolia*), one plant.
7 Goatsbeard (*Aruncus dioicus*), one plant.
8 *Astilbe arendsii* hybrids, two plants.
9 Bergenia (*Bergenia cordifolia*), one to two plants.

Planting the Background

Ferns tolerate shade and look attractive throughout the entire growing season. Look for variations in height and leaf and growth form.

Male fern, ostrich fern, and other ferns with tall, bending fronds belong in back, while smaller ferns with smooth leaves (e.g., hart's tongue fern) go in front.

Large, light-colored fieldstones provide permanent contrast.

Planting the Foreground

Loosen up the foreground of the bed with flowering shade-loving plants and small shrubs. Astilbes with colorfully harmonized flowers provide a spot of color in spring. A small rhododendron offers an alternative. Unlike astilbes, it will keep its foliage during the winter, but it is appreciably taller. Bergenias as well as hostas accent the foreground with leaves and flowers.

EXPERT TIP
Ferns need plenty of water in summer.

CROSS-REFERENCE
Ferns pages 118–119

Green Coverings

Information in Brief

Plants to Use for Green Coverings

Fruit trees (apples, pears) for sunny walls

Ivy for shaded walls

Woodbine for walls and arbors

Clematis for arbors and trellises

Climbing roses for arbors, trellises, and sunny walls

Sweet peas, beans, or nasturtiums for wire fences

Planting Time for Woody Climbers

Fall or spring

Espaliered Fruit

Espaliered fruit trees on a sunny wall look very attractive and provide you with fruit while saving space. In "informal" espaliers, all the side shoots are fastened to the wall after the branches growing forward have been removed.

The Green-clad Garden Arbor

Arbors must be very solidly constructed, with strong supports and firm crossbeams, for climbing plants have considerable weight. Pressure-treated square lumber looks more formal than round natural wood. Place arbors covered with flowering plants at a clearly visible spot in the garden. With an avenue-like planting in the foreground (trees, shrubs, two parallel beds) you direct the eye and create spacious depths.

Include green vines in your plan, not in the form of monotonous green walls but as a lively element in themselves.

Vine-clad Walls

If the wall belongs to your neighbors, you first must get their permission to cover it with vines. A combination of evergreen ivy and deciduous wood-bine (Virginia creeper) is particularly rewarding. Choose a variegated form of ivy (green-white, green-yellow), which provides a color accent throughout the year. The Virginia creeper comes into its own in fall, when its leaves turn a wonderful dark red. Cut both plants back in fall so that neither gets the upper hand.

Flowering Trellis

Trellises with flowering plants close off the sides of a terrace or a sitting area, create free-standing eyecatchers, or upgrade a dull garden house with their colors. Experiment with plant combinations: Clematis harmonizes wonderfully with climbing roses that bloom at the same time. Regularly remove the dead shoots of the clematis so that the roses are not "crushed to death." Also old trees create very natural backgrounds for climbing roses and clematis.

Green and Blooming Fences

Even the most unattractive fence, including chain link, is improved by a suitable covering of growth. Hang light flower boxes on sturdy lattice fences and plant them with cascading flowers. Or sow annual vines in front of a wire fence (follow directions on the seed packet). Since annuals are transient, you can try new flower combinations year by year. Variously colored fragrant sweet peas, nasturtiums, or morning glories are very beautiful.

EXPERT TIP
Climbing plants on pillars or pyramids create accents.

CROSS-REFERENCES
Creating rooms pages 158–159
Climbing plants pages 140–145

Creating Shrub Beds

Information in Brief

Space Needed for Shrub Beds

Island beds at least 7 × 10 ft
(2 × 3 m)
Space-dividing beds 7 ft (2 m)
deep
Open hedges 7–13 ft (2–4 m)
deep

Flowering Shrubs

Chinese Witchhazel (February)
Turkish Filbert or European
hazel (March)
Forsythia (April)
Deutzia (May)
Roses (Wild roses, June)
Elder (July)
Spirea (August)
Hypericum (September)

Fruit-bearing Shrubs

Shadbush (July)
Clematis (October–December)
Wintercreeper (August–
December, depending on
variety)
Roses (August–December)
European Mountain Ash
(October–November,
depending on variety)
Common Snowberry (Sep-
tember–November)

The Open Hedge
As an alternative to a shrub bed, in
a small yard you can plant an open
hedge of several rows. Build up a
shallow earth wall, about 20 in (50
cm) high, along the property line.
It "lifts" the shrubs planted on the
outside up a little and improves privacy. Choose shrubs to rhythmically
vary in height and then plant them
at varying distances from the fence.

Rose Beds with Lavender
Old roses, above all, tend to grow
bare at the bottom. Cover these
unattractive places with lower plants.
Lavender offers a long-term solution.
Its gray-green foliage and the lavender-blue to pink flowers harmonize
beautifully with white, yellow, and
pink to red roses.

Shrub beds serve as decoration or as privacy screens depending on whether they are planted open or closed.

Shrub Bed as Space Divider

If the flower beds curving into the lawn are not planted with perennials but with medium-tall shrubs, the room-creating effect of these separating elements increases considerably. In smaller gardens a single, especially attractive shrub will work by itself. In larger gardens its better to plant three to five shrubs that vary in height, growth form, and flowering times in order to maintain interest all year round.

Combine the shrubs with underplanted shade-tolerant perennials for a summery picture.

Shrub Border as Screen for Privacy

Installed as screens, pergolas and trellises create compact green "walls." With a shrub bed or some shrubs that are growing in a flower bed, on the other hand, you can block a particular part of the view (e.g., the terrace or the window of a neighbor, or a nearby pathway). Thus your terrace remains "open," you can still see into your garden, and yet you protect your private sphere.

Spring in the Shrub Bed

With shrub beds you need a little patience until the first delicate leaves show on the shrubs in spring. Bridge this period with spring flowers that are planted under and between the shrubs (bulbs, tubers, perennials). Spring flowers profit from the higher level of light between the still-bare shrubs. By the time the shrubs have leaves and almost no more light reaches the ground, they have finished their growing season.

EXPERT TIP
A shrub is often more effective than a tree.

CROSS-REFERENCES
Planting shrubs pages 46–47
Shrubs plant portraits pages 122–139

Movable Gardens

Information in Brief

Nonwinter-hardy Container Plants

Agave, cannas, bougainvillea, fuchsia, mimosa, myrtle, New Zealand flax, oleander, palms, rock rose

Vines for Planters

Ivy (variegated varieties), Virginia creeper, glory flower, grapevine, moonflower

Spring Plants for Planters

Crocus, primulas, snowdrops, Anemone blanda, grape hyacinths, dwarf iris, dwarf narcissi, dwarf tulips, pansy (viola)

Summer Plants for Planters

Begonias, brachycome, flea-bane, sedum, monkey flowers (mimulus), geraniums, lewisia, petunias, common sorrel (colored leaves), verbenas, annual lobelia, allysum

Mediterranean Mood
Plants from the Mediterranean region, for example bougainvillea, citrus plants, herbs like lavender, thyme, and oregano, agaves and palms create a very special flair. Some, like bouganvillea, citrus, and palms do not tolerate the frosts of colder climates. They must be brought into the house during the winter. A greenhouse is ideal, but a cool, light place is also good for wintering over.

Make sure when you are selecting pots to have appropriate material (e.g., terra cotta) in the southern style.

Symmetrical Entryway Decoration
The paved entry area of a house is only rarely suitable for a planting. Here tub plants provide a very effective remedy. Symmetrically arranged plants, for example, to the left and right of the door, underline a geometrically simple pathway to the door. For plain door materials (steel, plastic) choose tubs of metal or lacquered wood. For rustic entryways natural stone, clay, and untreated wood work better.

The effectiveness of planters is based on the plants on the one hand, and on the attractive containers on the other.

Informal Entries

Don't shy away from combining many planters of various sizes with colorfully mixed plantings. Such luxuriant fullness goes wonderfully well on broad steps or landings, beside entrances or passages. As soon as a plant is past its prime, it is exchanged for another.

But only use planters or pots of the same style or there will not be a unified look.

Planters on the Terrace

In summer, when you sit on the terrace more often, it's nice to have flowers and fragrance nearby. Plant boxes and tubs with various plants of the season (offered at reasonable prices in the nursery). Create planters in different styles from time to time, with which, depending on your mood, you can conjure up Mediterranean or tropical flair, rustic charm, or baroque severity on the terrace.

Eyecatchers

The more unusual the plant container, the more strongly the eye will be drawn to it—at the end of a path, in the vanishing point of an arch. Frequent flea markets for old water containers, small barrels, wheelbarrows, metal kitchen sieves, stone troughs, or lacquered pots. Even worn-out rubber boots can serve as planters.

However, when you are using unusual plant containers, don't attempt very striking plantings. Rather, choose plants that underscore the effect of the container.

EXPERT TIP
Simple flowerpots are often the best choice.

CROSS-REFERENCES
Planting tubs pages 54–55
Plant portraits pages 82–145

The Herb Spiral

Information in Brief

Alternative or Additional Plants from Inside to Outside

Thyme, rosemary, winter savory, hyssop, fennel, lovage, mugwort, wormwood, burnet, chervil, pot marigold, lemon balm, borage, water mint

Tools

Spade
Shovel
Trowel
Bricklayer's trowel (with mortar)

Materials

Natural stone or frostproof bricks (more severe effect)
Pond form or plastic sheeting
Rubble with large stones
Humus
Sand
Cement

Time Expenditure

Several days

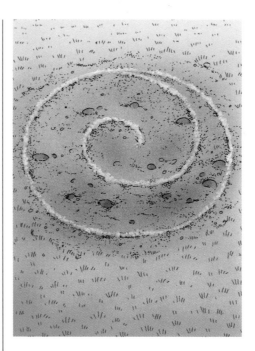

The Preparation

The location for the herb spiral must be sunny, since many herbs come from Mediterranean regions.

Make a circle of sand on the ground (diameter about 10 ft [3 m])—this constitues the outside boundary of the herb spiral. Then, starting in the east, sprinkle a narrowing spiral that ends in the west. Spring is the best planting time.

Laying Up Stones

Begin layering the stones for the wall (dry wall or mortared) in the center of the spiral. The edge should be about 30–39 in (75–100 cm) high and continually decrease in height until it gets down to one stone's height (in the south).

Be sure to make a stable wall, because it has to withstand the pressure of the soil when it is filled in.

You can use an herb spiral to plant kitchen herbs in the smallest amount of space and create a striking focal point in addition.

Filling In with Rubble and Stones

Fill in the center of the spiral up to half the "loop" with a mixture of rubble and stones so that water can drain away easily later. Over that comes a layer about 8–12 in (20–30 cm) deep of sand and soil.

Then the outer turns of the spiral are filled with soil. Toward the outside and underneath the soil may be somewhat "fatter." Finish off the herb spiral at the end with a small expanse of water.

Planting

Smooth the surface of the soil with a small rake. Since it is easily accessible from all sides, planting causes no difficulties. Begin in the center, and move from there to the outside. In the center plant the drought-tolerant plants; farther along toward the outside the moisture-requiring kinds have their place. Don't be afraid to loosen up the spiral with intermediate plantings of flowers (some rock garden perennials and nasturtiums will do here). Still, they should not only be useful but also look pretty.

Plant Plan

A possible sequence from outside to inside (moist to dry) would be:
Watercress (1, right by the water)
Sorrel (2)
Mint (3)
Chives (4)
Garlic (5)
Nasturtiums (6)
Dill (7)
Parsley (8)
Tarragon (9)
Lavender (10)
Marjoram (11)
Rock garden plant (12)
Sage (13)

EXPERT TIP
Put plants in the spaces of the dry wall.

CROSS-REFERENCE
Planting perennials pages 42–43

Paths in the Garden

Information in Brief

Path Underlay

Width of path 20–32 in (50–80 cm); deepen 6–10 in (15–25 cm) (depending on thickness of stones), and lay about 4 in (10 cm) of rubble plus 1 in (2.5 cm) of sand plus pathway paving

Path Materials

Bark mulch:
   Very simple to lay (for little-traveled paths even without underlay), very inexpensive
Gravel paths:
   Simple to install, inexpensive
Individual pavers:
   Easy to lay, relatively economical because of the small quantity
Bricks:
   Relatively simple to lay (lean cement), moderate price
Natural stone slabs:
   Difficult for the inexperienced to install (lean cement, cutting), expensive

Winding Gravel Paths

Gravel paths offer a good compromise between formal severity and naturalness. Winding gravel paths, in particular, have a natural look.

Gravel paths are easy to care for (raking), but over the course of the years they become somewhat unsightly. Replace the top layer of gravel then. In all cases secure the sides when laying the paths or you will kick the gravel into the beds or the field.

Nowadays gravel is not only available in different grain sizes but also in the colors gray, white, and red.

Natural Stone Slabs

Paths made of natural stone slabs are the best of all possibilities. They fit beautifully into any kind of garden landscape, are easy to walk on, and are stable. However, natural stone is very expensive and heavy to handle. It is not sold in standard sizes and must be cut to the correct dimensions (path turnings!). If the budget is small in the first few years after the house is built, better put off laying natural stone paths until later.

Chose the materials for the paths in your garden according to how much traffic the path gets and according to the style of the garden.

Bark Mulch Paths

Bark mulch decomposes over time and will not stand up to any heavy traffic. Bark mulch makes one of the best natural-looking pathways, almost reminding one of a forest. Therefore use these only for a natural garden.

Stepping-stones

If a stretch of path isn't used a great deal, stepping-stones are very appropriate. They fit into the lawn and are therefore practical.

However, be careful not to lay the stones along a precisely straight line.

Ornamental Paths

Very beautiful ornamental paths can be created by using a combination of various path materials (here wooden ties and paving stones) or by laying the paving material in a pattern. Then the paving itself becomes an artistic element in the garden composition. Limit yourself with striking or particularly artful patterns to prominent places like intersections, sitting areas, or bends in the path or you will direct the eye away from the plants too much.

Straight Paths

Straight paths, whatever material they are made from, direct the eye very strongly to a particular spot. Therefore, you should only use straight paths if you provide a visual focus at the same time. This can be a particularly pretty border, a gateway, a well, a sculpture, a plant container, a shrub or tree, or an arbor. This effect is increased with a symmetrical planting to the right and left of the path (e.g., two rose bushes, pillar yews, pruned boxwood).

EXPERT TIP
Make sure that bricks are made of frostproof material.

CROSS-REFERENCES
*Garden forms pages 12–13
Small shrubs pages 128–129*

Sitting Areas in the Garden

Information in Brief

Requirements for Sitting Areas

Daily use:
    Sunken sitting area, pergola
Weekend use:
    Sitting area on the lawn
    Sitting area under an arbor
Occasional use:
    Sitting area on the lawn
Primarily decorative element:
    Single bench

Space Requirements (minimum)

Single chair:
    3 × 3 ft (1 × 1 m)
Single bench:
    3 × 7 (10) ft (1 × 2 [3] m)
Bench in arbor:
    7 × 10 (13) ft (2 × 3 [4] m)
Pergola:
    10 × 10 ft (3 × 3 m)
Sunken sitting area:
    10 × 10 ft (3 × 3 m) or $11^1/_2$
    ft (3.5 m) in diameter
Round table with 4 chairs:
    $10–11^1/_2$ ft (3–3.5 m) in
    diameter
Rectangular table with 4 chairs:
    10 × 8 ft (3 × 2.5 m) in
    diameter

Sitting Areas on the Lawn
Anyone who prizes such a sitting area can naturally be very flexible. So long as the lawn does not constantly suffer heavy traffic, it can stand an occasional garden party without any problem.

However, be sure to regularly rotate chairs and table a little so that no deep depressions develop. Choose light, delicate furniture.

Sunken Sitting Areas
Only someone who is familiar with this kind of work (excavating, laying paving, masonry) should undertake making a sunken sitting area; if you are not, you are better off hiring an expert.

Decorate the walls around the edge with flowerpots and planters.

Permanently constructed sitting areas receive heavy wear and absolutely must be constructed by experts.

Single Bench

Since the single bench is often installed primarily as a decorative element, it pays to choose carefully. Cast-iron benches are charming, but not inexpensive. They can be painted strikingly (white, turquoise, or light-blue) or discreetly (dark-green or black).

Open Pergola

In addition to the purely functional aspect of a pergola, there is also the space-dividing effect. Not only must the view from the pergola be rewarding, the construction should also look pretty from a distance.

Bench in an Arbor

Such sitting areas invite whiling away some time. Here a person can read, carry on a good conversation or simply sit, look into the garden, and meditate.

Be especially careful choosing the bench. It should look nice and be comfortable at the same time.

Wooden benches fit into an arbor without any trouble; but they must be painted regularly with a protective chemical and need to be put someplace dry in the winter.

Sitting Areas by Water

This sitting area might become a meeting place for the family on hot days. The play of light on the water surface and the moving contours of plants in and near the water turn the sojourn by the pond into unalloyed pleasure.

Have such a sitting area—and the pond, if necessary—installed by an expert so that the weight will not injure the walls of the pond container.

Large stones or pieces of tree trunk are suitable for short-term sitting; they can be placed at appropriate spots along the banks.

EXPERT TIP
Former play areas are very suitable for turning into a sitting area.

CROSS-REFERENCES
Creating rooms pages 158–159
Climbing plants pages 140–145

Glossary of Technical Terms

Some of the technical terms used in the text are not well known to everyone and so are explained here.

Annuals: Plants that put out new growth from seed, form flowers and seeds, and then die. They are produced new every year from seed. Primarily this group includes summer flowers such as snapdragon, sweet alyssum, sweet peas, nasturtium, cornflowers, calendula, some mallows, impatience, nicotiana.

Arbor: Open garden building with pierced side walls; usually covered with green or flowering, rambling plants.

Ball: Earthen ball surrounding the root system of a plant.

Bed: Open surface that is planted with flowers or shrubs. A bed should be at least 5 ft (1.5 m) wide to allow room to play with and combine growth forms and colors. Shrub beds need even more space so that the shrubs can spread out to all sides and thus display to their best effect.

Biennial: Plants that put out new growth from seed in the first year but only develop flowers and seeds in the second. Among these are hollyhocks, English daisies, sweet Williams, wallflowers, forget-me-nots, foxglove, lunaria, and various thistle species.

Blood meal: Organic fertilizer from animal blood; very high in nitrogen content.

Blooming period: The phase in the life of a plant in which the flowers naturally develop. If flowers are regularly cut off after they have faded, there will often be a second blooming period.

Bone meal: Organic fertilizer produced from animal bones with a high phosphorus content.

Border: Special form of the perennial bed. Usually along a path or walls and fences.

Buds: Before growth, leaves, flowers, or side shoots are wrapped in involucral leaves. In this stage they are termed buds.

Bulbs: Storage organs of fleshy leaves that surround a resting stem. After they flower, the green leaves develop new nutrient supplies for the following year. Bulbs are planted in spring or fall according to the time of flowering. Familiar bulbs are tulips, hyacinths, daffodils, crocus, and narcissi.

Compost: Humus-like earth that is produced by composting of organic waste like leaves, weeds, and kitchen vegetable scraps; nutrient-rich spread for beds.

Conifers: Mostly evergreen woody plants whose leaves develop as needles. Familiar representatives of this woody plant group are fir, spruce, juniper, arborvitae, cypress, and pine. Conifers provide year-round green in the garden.

Container: Plastic pot for perennials, shrubs, and trees. Container plants can be planted all year long.

Corm, Tuber: Underground storage organ of perennials that consists of stems or roots. Tubers (e.g., dahlia) are used like bulbs and depending on the time of flowering are planted in spring (dahlias, gladiolas) or in fall (cyclamen).

Cottage garden bed: Lushly colorful bed interplanted with annuals, perennials, cooking and medicinal herbs in the style of farm or English cottage gardens. Suitable for small gardens.

Decomposition: The breakdown of organic waste with the help of soil organisms.

Dethatching: Using hand or motorized equipment, the turf is pierced vertically. This removes the thatch of matted roots and improves water drainage.

Dry wall: A layered, low wall of natural stone without mortar. Dryness-loving plants or herbs, such as thyme, sage, houseleek, and hens and chickens, can be planted in the earth-filled spaces between the rock courses.

Eye: Small, "sleeping" (dormant) buds, the eyes, are situated in the leaf axil of perennials, shrubs, and trees. Side branches develop from these.

Fertilizer, organic: Naturally occurring fertilizers like manure, blood meal, bone meal, hoof and horn, and seaweed. It gives up its nutrients to the soil slowly.

Fertilizer, chemical: Industrially produced fetilizer that contains all (complete fertilizer) or particular chemicals (special fertilizer). It gives up its nutrients to the soil quickly (with the exception of slow release fertilizers) and in a targeted fashion; mostly sold in the form of granules. Chemical fertilizer usually works faster than organic fertilizer and is also often cheaper.

Foliage passage: Open passageway with arching or flat, closed top; usually covered with green or blooming, rambling plants.

Frond: Leaves of a fern.

Grafting: In particular, roses and fruit trees are sold as grafted forms. In the process the nursery splices a branch of a bred variety (scion) to a robust understock (rootstock or trunk of a wild form). Scion and understock continue growing together.

Green fertilizer: Cover crops that are sown on an open area to improve soil structure and fertility. They prevent soil erosion, drying out of the soil, and suppress weeds (see Legumes).

Hoof and Horn meal: Organic fertilizer produced from cattle horns; fertilizer has a high nitrogen and

phosphorus content. The fine horn meal gives up its nutrients faster than the coarser horn shavings.

Humus: Nutrient-rich upper soil layer that consists of rotted organic material (see Compost).

Legumes: Plant group living in partnership (symbiosis) with soil bacteria (nitrogen-fixing bacteria). They can convert the nitrogen in the air into organically compounded nitrogen; good green fertilizers. The group includes such plants as beans, peas, sweet peas, all clover species, lupines, and yellow vetch.

Mulch: Covering layer for beds and open soil areas; mulch retains soil moisture, suppresses weeds, and provides winter protection to plants. Mulch material can be grass cuttings, leaves, ground up bark, and branches.

Nutrients: Soil minerals that are required for the growth of the plant, including nitrogen, phosphorous, and potassium.

Perennial (herbaceous): Flowering plants living for many years whose above-ground parts die back in winter (woody perennials, however, do not die back). Among these are catmint, sage, delphinium, peony,

CROSS-REFERENCES
Fertilizing pages 22–23
Composting pages 32–33

lupine, yarrow, gloriosa daisies, phlox, campanula, monkshood, fall asters.

Pergola: Open timber construction without any sides, such as over a terrace or a sitting area; often covered with climbing plants.

pH value: Indicates the acidity or alkalinity of the soil. Soils with a pH around 7 are neutral; lower values indicate soil is acid (e.g., peaty soils), higher values indicate alkaline soil (e.g., chalky soils). Majority of garden plants prefer a slightly acidic soil.

Shrub: Woody plant with several main shoots, which branch into side shoots; for example, forsythia, hazel, flowering quince, euonymus, weigelia, lilac, rhododendron.

Shrub bed: Beds that are planted with shrubs. The spaces in between are used for bulbs in spring, shade plants or ground covers in summer.

Side shoots: Develop from the bud of the main shoot. As a rule they bear the flowers.

Sogginess: In depressions or soils with a deep-lying layer of clay, the rain water cannot drain off and remains between the soil layers, resulting in sogginess.

Spent: As soon as the flower petals wither, the nutrient-consuming process of seed and fruit formation begins. If spent flowers are removed regularly, the plant usually "invests" in a new flower.

Terminal or apical bud: Bud located at the tip of a stem or branch. These buds are pinched off to promote a bushier habit in many plants.

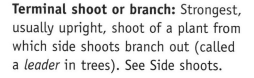

Terminal shoot or branch: Strongest, usually upright, shoot of a plant from which side shoots branch out (called a *leader* in trees). See Side shoots.

Tree: Woody plant with a main stalk from which all the side shoots branch out.

Useful plants: Vegetables, lettuce, seasoning and medicinal herbs, also fruit trees, indispensable in the kitchen garden.

Wild shoot: In grafted woody plants sometimes a so-called wild shoot grows out of the understock. It must be removed.

Woody plants: Plants with woody stems and branches (trees and shrubs).

Helpful Addresses

Help and suggestions for all gardening problems are offered by organizations and clubs, magazines and books. For written questions always include a stamped, self-addressed envelope.

Soil Testing:
Government Cooperative Extension Agencies:
For more comprehensive soil testing, contact your local government cooperative extension agency. It is a free source of information for all your gardening questions and problems including disease, pest control, and safe pesticide and herbicide recommendations.

Organizations/Societies
American Horticultural Society
7931 E. Boulevard Drive
Alexandria, VA 22308
(800/777-7931; 703/768-5700)

American Society of Landscape Architects
4401 Connecticut Avenue, NW, 5th Fl.
Washington, D.C. 20008-2302
(202/686-2752)

Canadian Plant Conservation Program
c/o Devonian Botanic Garden
University of Alberta
Edmonton, Alberta, Canada T6G 2E1

Garden Club of America
598 Madison Avenue
New York, NY 10022.

The Gardeners of America
5560 Merle Hay Road
Johnston, IA 50131-0241
(515/278-0255)

National Council of State Garden Clubs
4401 Magnolia Avenue
St. Louis, MO 63110-3492
(314/776-7574)

National Gardening Association
180 Flynn Avenue
Burlington, VT 05401
(802/863-1308)

National Junior Horticultural Association
1424 N. 8th Avenue
Durant, OK 74701-2602
(405/924-0771)

Ontario Horticultural Association
RR #3, Englehart, Ontario, Canada P0J 1H0
(705/544-2474)

United States Department of Agriculture (USDA)
6303 Ivy Lane, Room 400
Greenbelt, MD 20770
(301/344-2956)

Mail Order
Adirondack Designs
350 Cypress Street
Fort Bragg, CA 95437
(707/964-4940; 800/222-0343)
furniture

Alberta Nurseries & Seed Company
P.O. Box 20
Bowden, Alberta, Canada T0M 0K0
(403/224-3544, F. 224-2455)
plants, seeds, supplies

Bear Creek Nursery
P.O. Box 411
Northport, WA 99157-0411
plants, tools

Bluestone Perennials
7211 Middle Ridge Road
Madison, OH 44057
(800/852-5243)
extensive perennial selection, free catalog

D.V. Burrell Seed Growers Company
P.O. Box 150
Rocky Ford, CO 81067-0150
(719/254-3318; F: 254-3319)
seeds, books, supplies, tools

W. Atlee Burpee Company
300 Park Avenue
Warminster, PA 18974
(215/674-4900; 800/888-1447)
plants, seeds, bulbs, books, supplies, tools

Carroll Gardens
P.O. Box 310
444 E. Main Street
Westminster, MD 21158
(410/848-5422; 800/638-6334)
plants, books, tools

Pinetree Garden Seeds
P.O. Box 300
Gloucester, ME 04260
(207/926-3400)
annual and perennial flower and vegetable seeds, free catalog

Plants of the Southwest
Route 6, Box 11A, Agua Fria
Santa Fe, NM 87501
(505/471-2212; 438-8888)
plants, seeds, books

Taylor Ridge Farm
P.O. Box 222
Saluda, NC 28773
(704/749-4756)
arbors, trellises

E-Mail
Agropolis, The Texas A&M University System Agriculture Program:
http://agcomwww.tama.edu/agcom/agrotext/visitor.html

America On-line: The Garden Spot. Access through AOL's hobby files.

Garden Gate on Prairienet:
http://www.prairienet.org/ag/garden/homepage.htm

Gardening Sites:
http://www.ag.uiuc.edu/%7Edwardt/garden.htm

GardenNet:
http://www.olympus.net/gardens/welcome.htlm

The National Gardening Association:
http://www.wowpages.com/nga/

Ohio State University's WebGarden:
http://hortwww-2.ag.ohio-state.edu/hvp/webgarden/webgarden.html

For Further Reading

Selection of special literature about general garden care and garden design

The Anderson Horticultural Library's Source List of Plants and Seeds, 4th ed. Compiled and edited by Richard T. Isaacson, et al. University of Minnesota, 1996.

Barton, B. J., *Gardening by Mail*. New York: Houghton Mifflin, 1994.

Brooks, J., *The Book of Garden Design*. New York: Macmillan, 1991.

Bunemann, and Becker, *Roses*. Hauppauge, New York: Barron's, 1994.

Clarkson, R. E., *Magic Gardens*. New York: Macmillan, 1992.

Damrosch, B., *The Garden Primer*. New York: Workmen Press, 1988.

Ellis, B. and F. M. Bradley, eds., *The Organic Gardener's Handbook of Natural Insect and Disease Control*. Emmaus, PA: Rodale Press, 1992.

Fell, D., *Essential Bulbs: The 100 Best for Design and Cultivation*. New Jersey: Outlet Book Co., 1989.

Gibson, M., *Growing Roses for Small Gardens*. Portland, OR: Timber Press, 1991.

Heffernan, M., *Burpee Seed Starter*. New York: Macmillan, 1997.

Heitz, H., G. Jankovics, and U. Dorner. *Container Plants*. Consulting Ed. Dennis W. Stevenson. Hauppauge, NY: Barron's, 1992.

Heriteau, J., *National Arboretum Book of Outstanding Garden Plants*. New York: Simon & Shuster, 1990.

Hertle, Kiermeier, Nickig, *Garden Flowers*. Hauppauge, NY: Barron's, 1994.

Kremer, B.P. *Shrubs in the Wild and in Gardens*. Consulting Ed. Dennis W. Stevenson. Hauppauge, NY: Barron's, 1995.

Simon, H., *Gardening for Pleasure*. Hauppauge, NY: Barron's 1997.

Verey, R., *The Art of Planting*. Boston: Little, Brown, 1990.

Williams, R. *The Garden Planner*. Hauppauge, NY: Barron's, 1990.

Zeigler, C., *The Harmonious Garden*. Portland, OR: Timber Press, 1996.

Magazines/Newsletters

American Gardener
American Horticultural Society
7931 East Boulevard
Alexandria, VA 22308-1300
(free with membership)

The Avant Gardener
Horticultural Data Processors
P.O. Box 489
New York, NY 10028

Beautiful Gardens
CMK Publishing
P.O. Box 2971
Dublin, CA 94568

Fine Gardening Magazine
Taunton Press, Inc.
63 South Main Street
P.O. Box 355
Newtown, CT 06470

Garden Design
Evergreen Publishing Co.
4401 Connecticut Avenue, NW, Ste. 500
Washington, D.C. 20008-2302

Horticulture
98 N. Washington Street
Boston, MA 02114

The Landscape Architect Specifier News
2138 South Wright Street
Santa Ana, CA 92705

Organic Gardening
Rodale Press
33 East Minor Street
Emmaus, PA 18098

Index and Register of Species

The page numbers set in **boldface** indicate color photos and drawings.

Photo Credits

Baumjohann: page 48 top right, 49 left top, left bottom; Becker: pages 4–5, 10–11, 56–57, 76 top center, 89, 96 center, 99 center, 102 left, 109 left, 119 right, 124, 125 right, 127 right, 129 left, 137, 138 left, 139, 151, 152 right, 153 left, center, 169 right, 173 center, 178 right top, bottom, 179 left bottom, center; Borkowski: page 81; Borstell: pages C1, 6 right, 7 bottom left, bottom right, 8–9, 12, 14, 20–21, 31, 34–35, 44 bottom, 48 bottom, 76 bottom, 77 center top, center bottom, bottom, 78–79, 106–107, 114–115, 122–123, 129 center, 134–135, 140–141, 146–147, 152 left bottom, 155 left, 156, 164, 170 top left, bottom 171 right, 172 left, 173 left, right bottom, 177 left top, right, C4; Gardena: page 62 bottom left; Henseler: page 60 top, bottom; Himmelhuber: page 24 center top, bottom, 69 left top, left bottom, right; IPO: pages 19 right, 26 top left, top right, center; Kögel: page 13, 15, 77 top, 163, 169 center, 171 center, 172 right, 179 right; Kremer: page 24 center bottom, 25 top; mein schöner Garten (msG)/Jarosch: page 45 left bottom, 180; msG/Franke: page 39 center bottom; msG/Kögel: page 7 bottom center, 147 right; msG/Krieg: page 182; msG/Nordheim: page 47 center; msG/Stork: page 16 top, 27 right, 33 center, 36, 40 bottom, 48 top left, 49 center, right, 59, 158 bottom, 162, 168 bottom; Morell: page 131 right; Nickig: pages 7 top, 44 top, 76 center bottom, 84–88, 90, 91, 94, 95, 96 left, right, 97, 98, 99 right, 100, 101, 102 right, 103–105, 108, 109 center, right, 110–113, 116–118, 119 left, center, 120, 121, 125 left, center, 126, 127 left, center, 128, 129 right, 130, 131 left, center, 132, 133, 136, 138 center, right, 142–145, 152 left top, 153 right, 154, 155 center, right, 159 right, 168 top left, top right, 169 left, 173 right top, 176 right, 177 center, 184; Redeleit: pages 16 center top, center bottom, bottom, 17, 18 top left, top right, 19 left, center, 26 bottom, 27 left, center, 32, 33 left, right top, right bottom, 37, 38, 39 left, center top, right, 40 top left, top right, 41–43, 45 left top, center, right, 50–55, 58, 62 top right, bottom, 63, 64 left, 65, 68 left, 70–73, 75; Reinhard: pages 24 top, center, 25 center top, center bottom, bottom, 82–83, 159 left, 177 left bottom; Sammer: pages 64 right, 68 right, 69 center; Schaefer: pages 60 center top, center bottom, 61; Schlaback–Becker: page 176 left; Schneiders, U: pages 76 top, 92–93; Seidl: pages 99, 148–149; Stork: pages 6 left, 9 right, 18 bottom left, bottom right, 22, 23, 46, 47 left, right; Strauss: pages 150, 158 top left, top right, 159 center, 160–161; Tschakert: pages 170 top right, 171 left, 178 top left, 179 top left.

Published originally under the title:
Gartenspass für Einsteiger
© 1998 by Gräfe and Unzer Verlag GmbH. München
English translation © 1999 by Barron's Educational Series, Inc.

English translation by Elizabeth D. Crawford

All inquiries should be addressed to:
Barron's Educational Series, Inc.
250 Wireless Boulevard
Hauppauge, New York 11788
http://www.barronseduc.com

Library of Congress Catalog Card No. 98-37136

International Standard Book No. 0-7641-5164-9

Library of Congress Cataloging-in-Publication Data
Hensel, Wolfgang.
[Gartenspass für Einsteiger. English]
    Gardening for beginners : successful gardening—how to do it, important chores step by step / Wolfgang Hansel ; more than 350 color photographs by Ursel Borstell...[et al.] ; illustrations by Renate Holzner ; translation from the German by Elizabeth D. Crawford.
        p.   cm.
    Includes bibliographical references (p.   ) and index.
    ISBN 0-7641-5164-9
    1. Gardening.   I. Title.
SB453.H39813   1999
635.9—dc21   98-37136
                                    CIP

Printed in Hong Kong
9 8 7 6 5 4 3 2 1

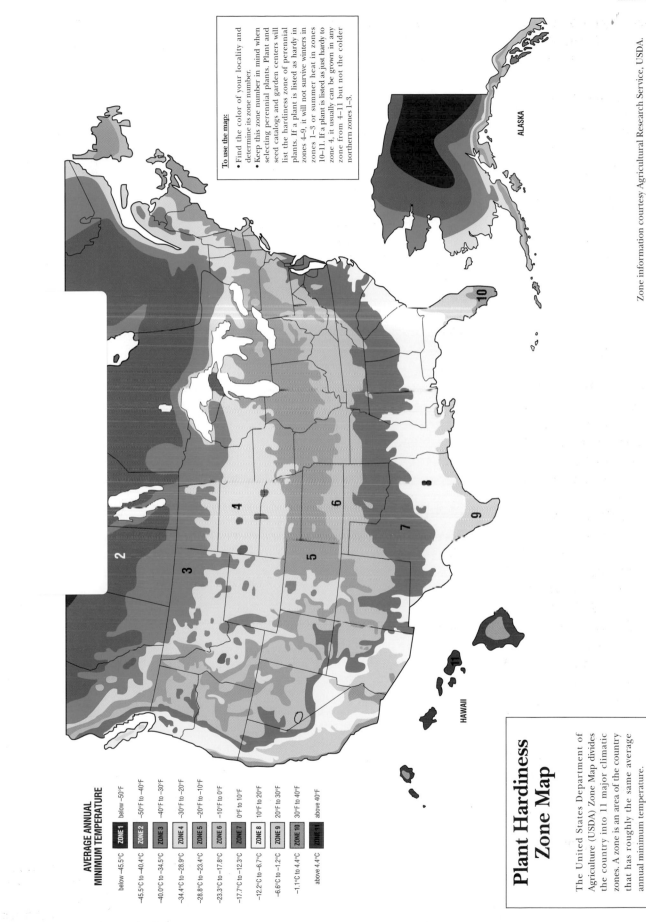

To use the map:

- Find the color of your locality and determine its zone number.
- Keep this zone number in mind when selecting perennial plants. Plant and seed catalogs and garden centers will list the hardiness zone of perennial plants. If a plant is listed as hardy in zones 4–9, it will not survive winters in zones 1–3 or summer heat in zones 10–11. If a plant is listed as just hardy to zone 4, it usually can be grown in any zone from 4–11 but not the colder northern zones 1–3.

ALASKA

HAWAII

Zone information courtesy Agricultural Research Service, USDA.

AVERAGE ANNUAL MINIMUM TEMPERATURE

ZONE 1	below –45.5°C	below –50°F
ZONE 2	–45.5°C to –40.4°C	–50°F to –40°F
ZONE 3	–40.0°C to –34.5°C	–40°F to –30°F
ZONE 4	–34.4°C to –28.9°C	–30°F to –20°F
ZONE 5	–28.8°C to –23.4°C	–20°F to –10°F
ZONE 6	–23.3°C to –17.8°C	–10°F to 0°F
ZONE 7	–17.7°C to –12.3°C	0°F to 10°F
ZONE 8	–12.2°C to –6.7°C	10°F to 20°F
ZONE 9	–6.6°C to –1.2°C	20°F to 30°F
ZONE 10	–1.1°C to 4.4°C	30°F to 40°F
ZONE 11	above 4.4°C	above 40°F

Plant Hardiness Zone Map

The United States Department of Agriculture (USDA) Zone Map divides the country into 11 major climatic zones. A zone is an area of the country that has roughly the same average annual minimum temperature.

A Walk Through the Garden Center

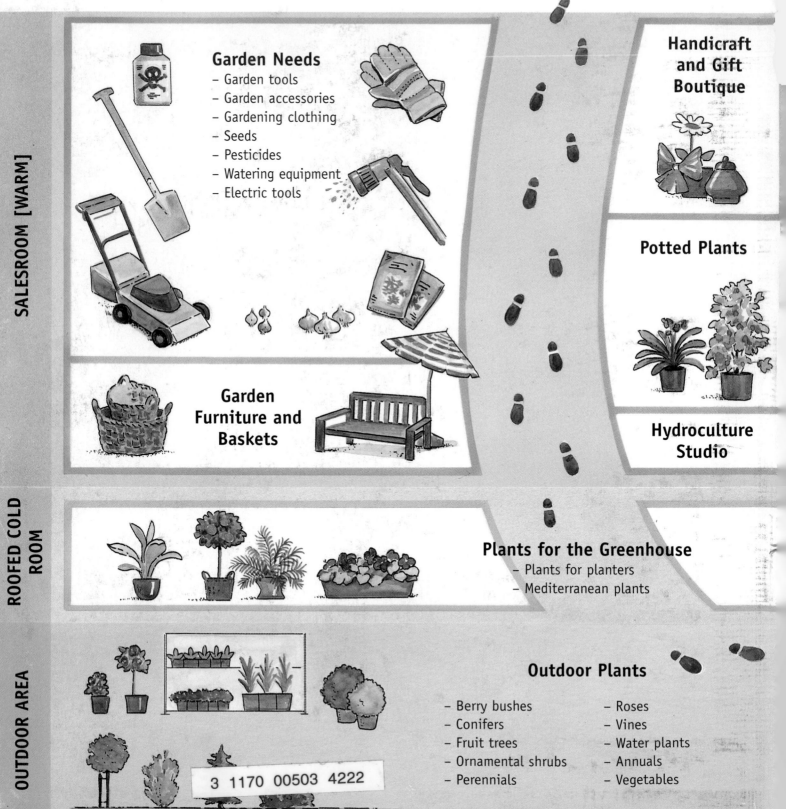

SALESROOM [WARM]

Garden Needs
- Garden tools
- Garden accessories
- Gardening clothing
- Seeds
- Pesticides
- Watering equipment
- Electric tools

Garden Furniture and Baskets

Handicraft and Gift Boutique

Potted Plants

Hydroculture Studio

ROOFED COLD ROOM

Plants for the Greenhouse
- Plants for planters
- Mediterranean plants

OUTDOOR AREA

Outdoor Plants
- Berry bushes
- Conifers
- Fruit trees
- Ornamental shrubs
- Perennials
- Roses
- Vines
- Water plants
- Annuals
- Vegetables

3 1170 00503 4222